THE BOOK
OF MARK

Other Books by Thomas R. Shepherd

Unmistakably Christian

THE BOOK OF MARK

Thomas R. Shepherd

 Pacific Press®
Publishing Association

Nampa, Idaho | www.pacificpress.con

Cover design by Brandon Reese
Cover design resources: Lars Justinen

The author assumes full responsibility for the accuracy of all facts and quotations as cited in this book.

Additional copies of this book are available for purchase by calling toll-free 1-800-765-6955 or by visiting AdventistBookCenter.com.

ISBN 978-0-8163-6998-0

January 2024

Dedication

To Robert M. Johnston, emeritus professor
of New Testament and Christian Origins,
Andrews University, Seventh-day Adventist
Theological Seminary. Teacher, missionary,
Doktorvater, and friend.

Contents

Introduction

The Gospel of Mark is the shortest of the four Gospels in the Bible. It does not contain the Sermon on the Mount, as Matthew does. It does not have the parable of the prodigal son, as Luke does. And it does not include the raising of Lazarus, as John does. There is no birth narrative and few parables, and it contains the least words spoken by Jesus recorded in any of the Gospels. So why study Mark?

One reason is that this Gospel is considered, by many scholars, to be the first one written. Studying the possible first book that documented the life, death, and resurrection of Jesus provides an early glimpse into the record of His ministry. Mark's story presents Jesus in bold strokes as He quickly moves from place to place. His miracles are striking attacks on Satan's realm as He casts out demons and raises the dead. He confronts religious leaders and even is misunderstood by His own family (Mark 3). He says some unusual things:

- "Who touched my garments?" while He is in the midst of a crowd (Mark 5:30).
- "The child is not dead but sleeping" (verse 39).

He also minces no words in rebuking unbelief:

- "Why are you so afraid? Have you still no faith?" (Mark 4:40).
- " 'If you can'! All things are possible for one who believes" (Mark 9:23).

This is not a Gospel with a meek-and-mild Jesus.

The first time I read Mark seriously, I was surprised to see that Jesus was different from what I expected. I was in the tenth grade, and to that point, I suppose I had more of a meek-and-mild view of Jesus. But Mark confronted me with a Jesus who was bold, forthright, and very powerful.

To some readers, His disciples come across as somewhat dense. But this is partly related to the Evangelist giving us inside knowledge of just who Jesus is from the very beginning: "The beginning of the gospel of Jesus Christ, the Son of God" (Mark 1:1). We know who Jesus is well before the characters in the story do. But their stumbling along behind Jesus helps us hear the Master's instruction to them, and if we have ever felt weak or in the dark, it is not so hard to identify with them.

The Gospel of Mark does have some surprises along the way. Why does Jesus always tell people to keep His Messiahship a secret? How do the demons know Him so well? Where is He going, and should we follow? The book does not offer much commentary about these questions. It seems that the author felt we would benefit more by seeing Jesus in action rather than having him tell us what it all meant. There is a surprise at the end of the book, but I will not ruin the fun of discovering that for yourself.

My academic study of Mark began during my master's and doctoral studies at the Andrews University Seventh-day Adventist Theological Seminary. I remember sitting in Dr.

Introduction

Robert Johnston's Mark class and hearing about Markan "sandwich" stories for the first time. I had never heard of this literary technique before. Dr. Johnston noted how two intertwined stories interpreted each other. Intrigued, I decided to make this the subject of my doctoral dissertation. And thus, I became a Mark scholar.

I have worked with the Society of Biblical Literature on the Gospel of Mark for more than twenty years and am the author of the new Seventh-day Adventist International Bible Commentary on this beautiful Gospel. It is my hope that this companion book to the Sabbath School quarterly will enrich your study of the Gospel of Mark.

1

The Beginning of the Gospel

When we go to a bookstore to find a good book to read, we often look for something by a particular author, knowing that person writes well. It may be a bit surprising, therefore, to realize that the four Gospels in our Bibles never mention the names of their authors in the text of these books. The Gospel that comes closest to naming the author is the Gospel of John, but even there, the author is simply known as "the disciple whom Jesus loved" (John 21:20–24).

However, in every case where we have the beginning of one of these books in the earliest manuscripts, the titles always include a proper name: "The Gospel according to Mark" (or Matthew, Luke, or John) or simply "according to Mark."

Who was Mark?

Mark was a common name in the Roman Empire, so we cannot be sure which Mark wrote the Gospel with his name attached.[1] But early church tradition—some of it going back to the second century—links the book with the Mark connected with the apostle Peter (1 Peter 5:13).[2] Irenaeus, writing in the second century, states: "Matthew also issued a written Gospel among the Hebrews in their own dialect, while Peter and Paul were preaching at Rome, and laying the foundations of the Church. After their departure, Mark, the disciple and interpreter of Peter, did also hand down to us in writing what had been preached by Peter."[3]

In the fourth century, Eusebius gives more details about Mark's ministry and references Papias, from the second century, as one of his sources:

> But a great light of religion shone on the minds of the hearers of Peter, so that they were not satisfied with a single hearing or with the unwritten teaching of the divine proclamation, but with every kind of exhortation besought Mark, whose Gospel is extant, seeing that he was Peter's follower, to leave them a written statement of the teaching given them verbally, nor did they cease until they had persuaded him, and so became the cause of the Scripture called the Gospel according to Mark. And they say that the Apostle, knowing by the revelation of the Spirit to him what had been done, was pleased at their zeal, and ratified the scripture for study in the churches. Clement quotes the story in the sixth book of the *Hypotyposes*, and the bishop of Hierapolis, named Papias, confirms him. He also says that Peter mentions Mark in his first Epistle, and that he composed this in Rome itself.[4]

It is not unreasonable to assume that the person referred to as John Mark in the book of Acts is the person who wrote the Gospel of Mark. He is first mentioned in Acts 12:12 as the son of a woman named Mary, who is evidently a wealthy patron of the church.

This same young man became a traveling companion of Paul and Barnabas on their first missionary journey (Acts

13:1–13). But after their experience in Cyprus with the Jewish false prophet named Bar-Jesus (also called Elymas), Mark decided to return to Jerusalem (verse 13). Luke gives no reason for this, but it seems that he returned because of discouragement at the difficulty of the missionary trip.[5] Reading between the lines, we might surmise that a young man used to an upper-class lifestyle would not be up to the rigors of a missionary journey in the first century. Perhaps it was his first time away from home, and he got more than he bargained for. In any case, he was a failed missionary.

But Barnabas, meaning "son of encouragement" (Acts 4:36), saw hope for the young man and wanted to take him along on the next missionary journey. This led to quite a row with Paul, who did not want to take a failed missionary with him on another trip (Acts 15:36–41). The two seasoned men separated over this disagreement, but God used the unfortunate incident to create two missionary teams in the place of one. Paul took Silas and went to Syria and Cilicia, and Barnabas took Mark and went to Cyprus—the very place Mark had left earlier to return home. Barnabas lived up to his name. Mark was rehabilitated to the point where the apostle Paul wanted him to be part of his team, writing to Timothy years later, "Get Mark and bring him with you, for he is very useful to me for ministry" (2 Timothy 4:11; cf. Colossians 4:10; Philemon 23, 24).

It is striking that a man who failed early in his experience eventually regained his footing to the point that he was useful and endeared to both the apostle Paul and the apostle Peter. Since he is likely the author of the Gospel of Mark, we might wonder if any telltale signs of his experience of failure and rehabilitation emerge in his story of Jesus. Indeed, it appears that we see such signs.

In this Gospel, the apostle Peter has an initial link and bond with Jesus that leads him to confess his Master as the

Messiah and insist that he will be faithful unto death (Mark 14:29). Unfortunately, he fails miserably in his promise (verses 66–72). But at the end of the Gospel, Peter receives a special message, not reported in any other Gospel, as expressed by the "young man" (angel) at the empty tomb: "But go, tell his disciples *and* Peter that he is going before you to Galilee. There you will see him, just as he told you" (Mark 16:7; emphasis added).

It all sounds similar to the experience of the young John Mark, who showed interest in being a missionary for Jesus, only to fail and return home but then be reinstated and rehabilitated for ministry. Note how this compares with Ellen White's description of the writers of the Bible: "The Creator of all ideas may impress different minds with the same thought, but each may express it in a different way, yet without contradiction. The fact that this difference exists should not perplex or confuse us. It is seldom that two persons will view and express truth in the very same way. *Each dwells on particular points which his constitution and education have fitted him to appreciate.* The sunlight falling upon the different objects gives those objects a different hue."[6]

Thus, we suggest that John Mark's personal experience gave him special empathy for understanding the failure and restoration of Peter. This may have drawn him into a special relationship with the aged apostle: "Mark, my son" (1 Peter 5:13).

The beginning of the Gospel of Mark

The Gospel of Mark begins with an incomplete sentence (Mark 1:1–3). Many Bible translations make verse 1 a sentence of its own, even though it has no verb. But in Greek, the sentence, which is still incomplete grammatically, may actually extend through verse 3. It is a conversation between God the Father ("I," verse 2) and God the Son ("your," verse

2), couched in the language of three passages from the Old Testament—Exodus 23:20; Isaiah 40:3; and Malachi 3:1. Each of these verses contributes to the message, but Mark only refers to Isaiah: "As it is written in Isaiah the prophet" (Mark 1:2).[7] The reason for this focus on Isaiah has to do with a major theme of the Gospel of Mark—Jesus' ultimate destination.

This focus on movement—where Jesus is headed—is highlighted by the words "the way of the Lord" in verse 3, which come from Isaiah 40:3. In the book of Isaiah, this "way of the Lord" will be a new Exodus of God's people.[8] Jesus' ministry in Mark will open before His disciples this new direction in life. But the path will lead to a location they do not expect—the cross. It will be the place where Jesus' death becomes "a ransom for many" (Mark 10:45). However, the disciples first must come to recognize who He is before He can reveal the tragic reality of His destination.

The baptism of Jesus in Mark 1:9–11 is the vital commencement of His ministry. Present at this event are God the Father ("You are my beloved Son," verse 11); Jesus, God the Son; and God the Holy Spirit, descending in the form of a dove.[9] The presence of the Three Members of the Godhead together at the same event signals that this event is crucial for understanding Jesus' ministry in Mark's Gospel.

The meaning of Jesus' ministry continues to unfold in His temptation in the wilderness (verses 12, 13). Mark's report of the temptation in the wilderness is much shorter than the accounts of Matthew and Luke. Those Gospels tell of the three temptations and Jesus' response to them. Mark only gives the barest of details with no dialogue.

But what is surprising is the way in which Jesus appears as both a strong and weak character in the opening events of the Gospel story. Jesus is the One stronger than John the Baptist (verse 7). He will baptize with the Holy Spirit (verse 8). He is the One on whom the Spirit rests and is the beloved Son (verses 10, 11). But He is driven by the Spirit into the wilderness, is tempted by the devil, is ministered to by angels, and lives with the wild beasts (verses 12, 13).

Why this emphasis on strength and seeming weakness? It is the opening indication of where Jesus is headed—not to a throne but to a cross, not to cast out the Romans but to become the "ransom for many" (Mark 10:45), and not to rule but to serve (verses 42–45).

Preaching in Galilee

More of the meaning of Jesus' ministry unfolds in His preaching in Galilee. His message is simple and direct: "The time is fulfilled, and the kingdom of God is at hand; repent and believe in the gospel" (Mark 1:15). Jesus' message here has three parts: a reference to a time prophecy, the announcement of the kingdom of God, and a call to discipleship ("repent and believe").

The time prophecy in view is the beautiful seventy-weeks Messianic prophecy of Daniel 9:24–27. In many Bible translations, verses 25 and 26 reference an "anointed one." The Hebrew word is *māšîaḥ*, which is the word *Messiah*. The reason that many Bibles do not translate this as "Messiah" is because of scholars' belief that the text refers to Antiochus Epiphanes in the second century BC rather than to Jesus in the first century AD.

However, a historicist reading of Daniel leads to the clear application of this passage to Jesus and His relationship to His people. Daniel 9 points to the beginning of the seventy-weeks prophecy with the going forth of the decree to "restore and build Jerusalem" (verse 25).

Three decrees were given for this rebuilding: Cyrus in 537 BC, Darius I in 520 BC, and Artaxerxes 458/457 BC (Ezra 1:1–4; 6:1–12; 7:1–26).[10] It was the third of these decrees that restored the civil state in Palestine.[11] Marking from this time leads to a date of AD 27 for the baptism of Jesus.[12] Luke 3:1, 2 indicates that John the Baptist began his ministry in the fifteenth year of Tiberius Caesar, and while there are some complexities in determining this date, a good case can be made for it extending from AD 27 to AD 28.[13] Consequently, we believe that the prophecy was exactly fulfilled with the baptism of Jesus.

A striking parallel to this fulfillment of prophecy in Mark 1 is the first angel's message of Revelation 14:7. The angel says, "Fear God and give him glory, because the hour of his judgment has come, and worship him who made heaven and earth, the sea and the springs of water." The parallel to Jesus' gospel message is illustrated in the following table.

Parallels between Mark 1 and Revelation 14

Mark 1	Category	Revelation 14
Time fulfilled (Daniel 9)	*Time prophecy*	Hour of judgment (Daniel 7; 8)
Kingdom near	*Covenant promise*	Hour of judgment (cf. Daniel 7:22, 27)
Repent and believe the gospel	*Call to discipleship*	Fear, glorify, and worship God

Just as Jesus' preaching at the beginning of the gospel proclamation was a fulfillment of the seventy-weeks prophecy of Daniel 9, so the end-time preaching of the three angels' messages is a fulfillment of the great 2,300-day prophecy of Daniel 8, which parallels the judgment scene of Daniel 7. God comes to the rescue of His people: first, by sending His Son to die on the cross at the initiation of the gospel message; and at the end, with the preaching of the three angels' messages, which is a final call for people to worship their Creator and Judge.

1. See R. T. France, *The Gospel of Mark*, New International Greek Testament Commentary (Grand Rapids, MI: Eerdmans, 2002), 36, 37.

2. See Eusebius, *Church History* 2.15.1–2; 3.39.15; 6.14.5–7; Irenaeus, *Against Heresies* 3.1.1.

3. Irenaeus, *Against Heresies* (3.1.1), in vol. 1 of *The Ante-Nicene Fathers*, trans. Arthur Cushman McGiffert, ed. Alexander Roberts, James Donaldson, and A. Cleveland Coxe (Buffalo, NY: Christian Literature Pub., 1885), 414.

4. Eusebius, *Ecclesiastical History* (2.15.1–2), vol. 1, trans. Kirsopp Lake, Loeb Classical Library 153 (New York: G. P. Putnam's Sons, 1926), 143, 145.

5. Ellen G. White, *The Acts of the Apostles* (Mountain View, CA: Pacific Press®, 1911), 169, 170.

6. Ellen G. White, *Selected Messages*, bk. 1 (Washington, DC: Review and Herald®, 1958), 22; emphasis added.

7. The earliest and more reliable manuscripts have "As it is written in Isaiah the prophet." Later scribes noticed that the text references Exodus, Isaiah, and Malachi, and so shifted the wording to "As it is written in the prophets."

8. See Rikki E. Watts, *Isaiah's New Exodus in Mark*, Biblical Studies Library (Grand Rapids, MI: Baker, 2000), 89.

9. The Three Members of the Godhead—Father, Son, and Holy Spirit—are referred to together more than forty times in the New Testament. The doctrine of the Trinity is not a minor teaching of Scripture.

10. Francis D. Nichol, ed., *The Seventh-day Adventist Bible Commentary*, vol. 4 (Washington, DC: Review and Herald®, 1980), 925.

11. Nichol, *The Seventh-day Adventist Bible Commentary*, 4:925.

12. Seventy prophetic weeks times seven days in a week equals 490 years. The Messiah would come after sixty-nine prophetic weeks or 483 years: 483 years – 457 BC = AD 26. However, there is no year 0 between BC and AD; hence, the number 1 must be added to the AD year when crossing from BC to AD. Therefore, the sixty-nine weeks extend to AD 27.

13. Francis. D. Nichol, ed., *The Seventh-day Adventist Bible Commentary*, vol. 5 (Washington, DC: Review and Herald®, 1980), 242–248.

2

A Day in the Ministry of Jesus

I have lived on three continents: North America, Africa, and South America. One of the things I learned about my own North American culture was the surprising fact that people who have more "time-saving" devices seem to have much less time to spend with others. Busy, busy, busy. Too busy to talk, too busy to relax, always on the go, and lots and lots to do.

If this sounds like your life, welcome to the club. Modern life is hectic, and time-saving devices—phones, computers, and many other machines—have not decreased our workload. Life before the industrial age was slower, and people seemed to have more time for one another. But in reading the first chapter of Mark, it seems that Jesus had a very busy life. How did He handle all of that, and what kept Him calm?

A little background

Each of our four Gospels introduces the adult ministry of Jesus in a different way. Matthew famously presents the Sermon on the Mount (Matthew 5–7). Luke recounts Jesus' inaugural sermon in the Nazareth synagogue (Luke 4), noted for its inclusion of His gospel mission as described in Isaiah 61:1, 2. The words of Isaiah predict the agenda for His ministry throughout the book of Luke and, strikingly, the way some people will react to Him and His work. John presents Jesus calling the first disciples: Andrew, John, Peter, Philip, and Nathanael (John 1).

The Gospel of Mark introduces the inauguration of Jesus' ministry uniquely. It can be titled "A Day in the Life of Jesus" or "A Day in the Ministry of Jesus." It takes place on a Sabbath in Capernaum (Mark 1).

Mark, just sixteen chapters long, is the shortest Gospel. It features accounts where what is narrated occurs in an approximately twenty-four-hour period. In chapters 4 and 5, we find parables, a trip across the lake, the healing of a demoniac, a trip back across the lake, the healing of a woman, and the resurrection of Jairus's daughter—all in a span of about thirty-six hours. In chapter 8, there is the feeding of the four thousand, crossing the Sea of Galilee, arguing with some Pharisees, traveling back across the lake, instructing the disciples, and healing a blind man. In chapter 9, we find the Transfiguration and the healing of a demon-possessed boy. And finally, in chapters 11–16, the last week of Jesus' life is chronicled. Events include His coming to Jerusalem, dying on the cross, and rising from the dead. All told, the chapters that present a twenty-four-hour period or a continuous time of about one week amount to eleven of the sixteen chapters of the book!

What this suggests is that Mark tends to present us with vignettes of Jesus' ministry—windows on activities happening at key moments in His healing and saving work. This gives the book a strong sense of the reader being immediately present when all the action is taking place. It is a dramatic presentation, focusing on the actions and activities of Jesus rather than on His words. In fact, there are only two extended discourses of Jesus in the Gospel of Mark: the parables in chapter 4 and the eschatological discourse in chapter 13. The teachings of Jesus are important to Mark, but he seems to focus more on the actions of the Master.

Calling disciples

After a brief introduction to the ministry of John the Baptist and his interaction with Jesus (Mark 1:4–13), Mark turns to Jesus' initial ministry of preaching, healing, and calling His disciples. In Jesus' day, it was typical for those interested in learning from a rabbi to go and attach themselves to that teacher.[1] But Jesus does not follow that pattern. Instead, He calls the disciples to follow Him and "become fishers of men" (verse 17).

These disciples, and the others that join later, follow Jesus all through the Gospel of Mark. They experience the ups and downs, successes and failures, yet remain with Jesus to the end. In spite of their failures when He goes to Jerusalem, Jesus does not give up on them but chooses to meet with them in Galilee after His resurrection.

Because the disciples come across as a little bumbling, some scholars feel that the Gospel of Mark is a rejection of these men, even though they eventually become the leaders of the early Christian church. But such a view is mistaken for at least two reasons. First, Jesus does not give up on them, even when they make big mistakes; He meets with them after His resurrection (see Peter's denial in Mark 14:66–72, but Jesus calls for him to meet with Him in Galilee in Mark 16:7). Second, Jesus predicts that they will be His emissaries to the world after His resurrection (Mark 10:35–45; 13:9–13). All of this comes true, validating His acceptance of the disciples.

The training of the disciples comes in stages. Initially, Jesus does not foretell where the journey of discipleship will lead. He begins with a simple call to follow Him and a promise that the disciples will become fishers of men. He ends up choosing twelve men (Mark 3) and sends them on a preaching and healing mission (Mark 6). In Mark 8–10, He carefully teaches them about His coming death and resurrection, connecting these events with important truths for all His future disciples.

The special Sabbath

As I mentioned earlier, the evangelist tells about a day early in Jesus' ministry (Mark 1:21–39). It is a Sabbath day in Capernaum—a city situated on the northwestern edge of the Sea of Galilee. The Sea of Galilee is a small lake, approximately eight miles wide and thirteen miles long. While not too impressive as lakes go (Lake Superior in North America is 350 miles long and 160 miles wide), the Sea of Galilee is the largest body of fresh water in Palestine—a land characterized by a dry climate and few sources of water.

It is difficult to estimate just how many people lived in Capernaum in Jesus' day. Estimates run from sixteen hundred to ten thousand.[2] The area around Capernaum contains basalt, a dark igneous stone, and the residents of the town used basalt blocks to build their houses. Today one can see the lower courses of the basalt stone walls of homes when visiting the site. The ruins of a famous fourth-century AD synagogue, known as the White Synagogue, are still present in Capernaum. It is called the White Synagogue because of the light-colored limestone used in its construction. However, the foundation of the synagogue is the dark basalt stone of the local area. This has led to the proposal that the former synagogue, perhaps the one that Jesus preached in as described in Mark 1, was actually built earlier on the same spot.

An unforgettable experience occurs in the synagogue that Sabbath as a man with an unclean spirit accosts Jesus. His actions display the power struggle between the forces of evil and the forces of good. "What have you to do with us, Jesus of Nazareth? Have you come to destroy us? I know who you are—the Holy One of God" (verse 24).

The demon makes three statements. First, he questions what Jesus has to do with "us." "Us" probably refers to the demons that counter Jesus' work; however, someone sitting in the synagogue could easily think that the demon-possessed man is talking about the synagogue's congregation.

If the "us" is the congregation, then the next statement, if true, means that Jesus has come to destroy the people in the synagogue—maybe all the people of Capernaum. Such a perspective flies in the face of all that Jesus stands for in His relationship to people. He comes to heal and save humanity, not destroy it (Luke 19:10; John 3:16, 17).

The third statement by the demon places his other two statements in context. Jesus is the "Holy One of God," and of course, the demon is unclean. Jesus casts out such demons to bring relief and health to those who are tormented by the evil one. This confrontation in the synagogue illustrates the great-controversy theme in Mark, where Jesus stops demons from tormenting people and sets those people free to serve God. Therefore, the demon's recognition of Jesus as the Holy One of God indicates that Christ has come to destroy the devil and his evil angels, not the common people.

Jesus casts the demon out and tells it to be quiet (*phimoō*, "to muzzle, silence, put to silence"). The demon is depicted as an animal that needs to be tamed and muzzled. Jesus' words accomplish the task as the demon convulses the man, cries out with a loud voice, and departs. Silencing an evil spirit is certainly a work of the Messiah. But this reference to silence is one of the first indications of a motif that runs throughout the book—the revelation-secrecy motif.

The purpose of the secrecy in Mark is twofold. First, it helps to prevent Jesus' ministry from being shortened due to a popular uprising, which would likely cause the Romans to squash the movement. And second, it allows Jesus time to prepare His disciples for something they are not expecting—the cross. Jesus leads His disciples through steps of growth: first, calling them (chapters 1; 2); second, designating the Twelve (chapter 3); third, sending them on a mission (chapter 6); and fourth, teaching them about where He is headed (chapters 8–10). Their inadequacies give Jesus the opportunity to instruct them on the meaning of His mission, which allows Mark to share that teaching with his readers.

After the eventful meeting in the synagogue, Jesus retires to the house of Simon Peter. The text indicates that Peter's mother-in-law is sick (Mark 1:30). This immediately shows us that Peter is married. As is typical of the times, he likely has a number of children, so it might be a crowded home. Jesus is told that Peter's mother-in-law is sick with a fever. The fever could be caused by any number of diseases, but it debilitates her. Jesus simply takes her by the hand and raises her up, and the fever departs.

Mark notes in verse 32 that people come to Peter's house after sunset. The evangelist does not explain this specific time reference. It is an interesting detail that suggests the readers of his Gospel knew exactly what he meant—that the Sabbath extends to Saturday at sunset. The people of Capernaum may have been afraid that they would get in trouble with the religious leaders if they came during the Sabbath (cf. Luke 13:14). Mark does not have to explain why they waited until after sunset, indicating that he expected his readers to know about the Sabbath. Furthermore, it is consistent with these readers being Sabbath keepers themselves.

The secret of Jesus' success
What made Jesus so successful in His ministry? Mark 1 shows us at least one of the characteristics that made Jesus a man like no other. He was a man of prayer. Over and over

in the Gospels, we see pictures of Jesus praying and teaching His disciples to pray: Matthew 6:7–15; 14:23; 26:39, 42, 44; Mark 1:35; 6:46; 14:35; Luke 5:16; 6:12; 9:18, 28, 29; 11:1; 22:32, 41, 44, 45; John 17. Jesus' model prayers, such as the Lord's Prayer, present various characteristics of His ideal for prayer (Matthew 6:9–13; Luke 11:1–4; cf. John 17).

First, the focus is on God—His glory and His will. This emphasis always precedes the request for help with specific needs. Second, there is the simple expression of needs for God to fulfill. These are not expressed in flowery terms, just simple prose of physical and spiritual needs. Finally, there is the focus on reciprocal forgiveness—that is, asking God to forgive us just as we forgive others.

These details suggest our need to submit to the will of God, asking Him to supply our needs. The outpouring of God's grace changes the way we treat others around us. This kind of prayer has a calming effect on our lives, and God's Spirit shows us how to act toward others.

Years ago, I gave my students a prayer assignment. They could either read about prayer in the books *Steps to Christ* and *The Ministry of Healing* or spend thirty minutes in prayer—all at one time. Then they had to write a one-page report on the exercise they chose.

I received some amazing reports from those who spent thirty minutes in prayer. A number of students noted the calmness they felt after spending this extended time in prayer. Others told how they prayed their usual prayer for a few minutes and then did not know what to do. Others said that they eventually prayed for people they had not thought of in years.

The prayer assignment taught me a couple of lessons. First, prayer calms the spirit; and second, the shorter your prayers, the more you tend to pray about yourself. This makes me think that it was Jesus' extended periods of prayer that gave

Him such remarkable calmness throughout His ministry, making Him the greatest power for good the world has ever seen.

---

1. See Mark L. Strauss, *Mark*, Zondervan Exegetical Commentary on the New Testament (Grand Rapids, MI: Zondervan, 2014), 83.

2. See Henry I. McAdam, "*Domus Domini*: Where Jesus Lived (Capernaum and Bethany in the Gospels)," *Theological Review of the Near East School of Theology* 25, no. 1 (2004): 53; R. T. France, *The Gospel of Mark*, New International Greek Testament Commentary (Grand Rapids, MI: Eerdmans, 2002), 101.

3

Controversies

Controversy is difficult to handle. We naturally like peace and getting along with others. However, it is clear throughout the Gospels that Jesus did not get along with the religious leaders of His day. Why all the turmoil and disagreement? The reason is that what Jesus taught stood in sharp contrast with what the religious leaders taught. This difference shows up early in the Gospel of Mark when Mark notes that Jesus taught with authority, not like the scribes (see Mark 1:22). Jesus was clear in what He stood for. The scribes were not. Their traditions undermined the authority of the Word of God, and Jesus called them out on it.

Five controversy stories

The Gospel of Mark illustrates this atmosphere of conflict with two sets of conflict stories. They are concentrated in Mark 2 and 3, and Mark 11 and 12. In this chapter, we will focus on three of the five stories in Mark 2:1–3:6. They follow a concentric, or circle, pattern where each story deals with two topics or concepts, with one of these linking with the next story.[1] The last story links back to the first story in this manner. A table makes this clear:

Concentric pattern of controversy stories in Mark 2 and 3

Reference	Story	Concentric pattern
2:1–12	Paralytic	Healing/sin
2:13–17	Levi called	Sin/food
2:18–22	Fasting/feasting	Food/Messiah
2:23–28	Sabbath keeping	Messiah/Sabbath
3:1–6	Sabbath healing	Sabbath/healing

At the heart of these five controversies, the evangelist highlights truths about who Jesus is and what His authority entails. Each of these stories revolves around a biblical truth that is linked to Jesus. We can identify certain verses in these stories that emphasize these ideas.

Truths about Jesus in Mark 2 and 3

Story	Concept	What it tells us about Jesus
Paralytic man	2:10: "The Son of Man has authority on earth to forgive sins."	Jesus is the divine Son of God who can forgive sin.
Levi called	2:17: "Those who are well have no need of a physician, but those who are sick. I came not to call the righteous, but sinners."	Jesus is the spiritual Physician who can save sinners.
Fasting	2:20: "The days will come when the bridegroom is taken away from them, and then they will fast in that day."	The Messiah will go to the cross.
Sabbath breaking	2:28: "The Son of Man is Lord even of the Sabbath" (NIV).	Jesus has authority over the Sabbath to explain how it should be kept.

Sabbath keeping	3:4: "Is it lawful on the Sabbath to do good or to do harm, to save life or to kill?"	Jesus keeps the Sabbath and teaches that it is lawful to do good on the Sabbath.

Notice that all the verses highlighted in this table are the words of Jesus. He explains the stories' themes and their focus. The three stories we will examine are the story about the healing of the paralytic man, the story regarding fasting, and the story concerning the dispute over Sabbath breaking.

The paralytic

The opening of the story of the paralytic man indicates that Jesus had returned to Capernaum. Houses in Capernaum at that time were made of basalt stone.[2] The size of the rooms was limited by the usual size of tree limbs used as crossbeams, confining the width and breadth of a room to about fifteen feet. Thus, the room in which Jesus was teaching was not large. The crowd who came to hear Him spilled out onto the street. This made it next to impossible for the paralytic man's friends to bring him into Jesus' presence.

The four friends, and perhaps the man himself, came up with a novel plan to get him into Jesus' presence. They went up on the flat roof of the house and broke through the ceiling. This would not be a small task, though it would require less work than doing so in many houses today.[3] After making the opening, they lowered the paralytic man down in front of Jesus. The Lord saw their faith in Him through their earnest effort to get the paralytic man into His presence. But instead of immediately healing the man, Jesus told him that his sins were forgiven.

The controversy in this story centers around this statement. The scribes rightly hold that only God can forgive sins. Jesus' explicit statement that He has the authority to forgive sins implicitly teaches that He is the divine Son of God. He proves His point by healing the man's paralysis. The logic of the miracle-forgiveness linkage is that God will not heal through someone who is a blasphemer; hence, Jesus is who He claims to be. This outcome later leads the religious leaders to claim that Jesus casts out demons by the power of the devil (Mark 3:22). We will see in the next chapter how Jesus counters that charge.

Mark 2:10 is the first place in Mark where the phrase "Son of Man" is used. In the Gospels, this phrase always refers to Jesus, and in most instances, it is Jesus Himself who uses the term. The phrase links to Daniel 7:13, 14, where "one like a son of man" comes before God, the Ancient of Days, to receive a kingdom. In Jesus' day, this phrase had Messianic implications but did not necessarily have the nationalistic overtones that some other phrases did.[4] Jesus' use of the phrase is instructive because it implies that He is claiming to be the Messiah but not the Messiah that many in His day were expecting. This becomes clearer in the third controversy story regarding fasting.

The question of fasting

The central story of the five controversy stories revolves around a question about fasting (Mark 2:18–22). "Now John's disciples and the Pharisees were fasting. And people came and said to him [Jesus], 'Why do John's disciples and the disciples of the Pharisees fast, but your disciples do not fast?' " (verse 18).

The only day of fasting required by the Mosaic Law was the Day of Atonement (Leviticus 16:29, 30). But fasting was also done in times of famine and during periods of war or other crises. It was also used to lament calamities, to appeal to God in times of illness (Psalm 35:13; 2 Samuel 12:16), and to signal religious devotion.

John the Baptist's ascetic lifestyle was compatible with the practice of fasting, and his disciples obviously followed it, as this passage in Mark illustrates.

Just who posed the question to Jesus is unclear, but the query seems to suggest that the questioners were not the disciples of John or the Pharisees. If the Pharisees or John's disciples were asking the question, we might have expected them to say, "Why do *we* fast, but Your disciples do not?"

To answer the question about fasting, Jesus tells a little story about a wedding feast, a kind of parable, though it is not described as such. In His commentary, He states the obvious: it would be odd for guests at a wedding feast to abstain from food and drink. Here Jesus is identifying Himself as the Bridegroom and His disciples as the wedding guests. While He, the Bridegroom, is present, it is a time of rejoicing, not a time for crying and fasting.

But in the same breath, Jesus ominously points to a time when the Bridegroom will be taken away. Since we, as Christians, know where this is headed, we see a clear reference to His Passion: His arrest, trial, death, and resurrection. It is likely that those present only vaguely grasped what He meant, certainly not foreseeing the cross. This is one of the first references in the Gospel of Mark that points forward to the cross. It is brief, cryptic, and vague, but it is a signpost pointing to the way of the Lord, leading to the cross.

"Breaking" the Sabbath

In Mark 2:23–28, the first of two controversies over the Sabbath takes place. Everyone knows that the Sabbath commandment prohibits work: "On it you shall not do any work" (Exodus 20:10). But how do we define *work*? The commandment itself does not define what is included in *work*. In order to specify what was included in *work*, the

Jews prepared a list of thirty-nine activities, mainly revolving around daily tasks in an agrarian society.[5]

As Jesus' disciples were walking along one Sabbath day, they plucked heads of grain, rubbed them in their hands, blew away the chaff, and ate the grain. This would not be considered stealing since the Law allowed a person to assuage his or her hunger in a neighbor's field (Leviticus 19:9, 10; 23:22; Deuteronomy 23:24, 25). But the Pharisees suddenly ask Jesus why His disciples are breaking the Sabbath (Mark 2:24). While the Pharisees do not specify the exact offense, they are likely referring to the disciples plucking the grain (reaping), rubbing it in their hands (threshing), and blowing away the chaff (winnowing).

In Jesus' response to this attack, He cites the story of David eating the shewbread in 1 Samuel 21. It was lawful only for the priests to eat this bread, but the high priest obviously allowed David and his men to eat the bread on the basis that they were ceremonially clean. It was outside the regular pattern, but evidently, the high priest saw an acceptable exception in the case of David's need. Jesus' response is unique in that, typically, it was not considered appropriate to argue from a story for a ruling about a law. The usual method was to argue from a law.[6] But Jesus appears to be arguing typologically that He is parallel to David ("Son of David," Mark 10:47, 48) and His disciples are parallel to David's men.[7] If it was acceptable for David and his men, it was acceptable for Jesus and His disciples.

Jesus goes on to lay down an important principle concerning the Sabbath: "The Sabbath was made for man, not man for the Sabbath" (Mark 2:27). The Sabbath was created by God at the close of Creation week for the benefit of humanity. Humans were not created to serve the Sabbath. The Pharisees' complaint to Jesus was along the latter lines—that humans were constrained by the Sabbath instead of benefiting from it. Jesus brushes away this misunderstanding with His pronouncement concerning the meaning of the Sabbath. He verifies His pronouncement with the assertion that He is the Lord of the Sabbath (verse 28). This assertion has implications concerning Creation itself. It indicates that Jesus, as the Creator, can explain the meaning of the Sabbath.

Sandwich stories

The Gospel of Mark employs a unique storytelling pattern known as *sandwich stories* or, more technically, intercalations. One story is begun but then interrupted by another story that is told in full. Then the interrupted story is completed. This pattern appears at least six times in Mark: Mark 3:20–35; 5:21–43; 6:7–31; 11:12–25; 14:1–11, and 53–72.[8] The two stories are brought together but also held somewhat apart. Other than Jesus and His disciples, characters do not cross between the stories.

For instance, in Mark 3:20–35, Jesus' family does not appear in the inner story, and the scribes do not appear in the outer story. However, these story characters, who do not cross into each other's stories, do have a linkage to one another. In the sandwich stories, parallel characters do opposite actions, or opposite characters do parallel actions. In the outer story here in Mark 3, Jesus' family thinks He is crazy and tries to take control of Him. In the inner story, the scribes' parallel claim is that Jesus is possessed by the devil. Jesus' family should be on His side, but they appear to be allied with His opponents.

This tension produces dramatized irony, expressed in three ways: two levels of meaning, the two levels contrast each other, and someone who does not see the irony.[9] In this sandwich story, the two levels are the two stories, linked together but held apart. The contrast is the family of Jesus, who should be on His side, and the scribes, who are clearly His enemies.

The irony is that the family of Jesus is allied with His enemies, bringing similar charges against Him ("He is crazy," and "He has the devil").

A strange twist on this irony is that Jesus' family does seem to be divided from Him—"If a house is divided against itself, that house will not be able to stand" (verse 25)—and Jesus does argue in an unusual way in verses 23–27 where He contends that Satan's house cannot stand if it is divided against itself, but then He turns around and speaks of someone plundering a strong man's house (likely Jesus Himself, plundering Satan's kingdom). So, if Satan is divided, he will fall, but if he is attacked by someone stronger (Jesus), he will also fall. Jesus' argumentation does seem unusual, some might say crazy (like His family's accusation). Either way, Satan loses.

But Jesus resolves this seeming conundrum by redefining family in Mark 3:34, 35. His house is not divided: the disciples are His family. Satan's kingdom is not part of His family, and it is sure to fall. The lesson is unmistakable: Jesus will ultimately win, and we can be part of His family if we do God's will instead of resisting His truth.

---

1. See Joanna Dewey, *Markan Public Debate: Literary Technique, Concentric Structure, and Theology in Mark 2:1–3:6*, Society of Biblical Literature Dissertation Series 48 (Chico, CA: Scholars Press, 1980).

2. The Jordan River valley, with the Sea of Galilee at its upper end, forms part of the Great Rift Valley complex, which begins in eastern Africa and extends up through the Gulf of Aqaba and the Jordan Valley. Two tectonic plates converge at this point—the African plate and the Arabian plate. At such junctures, earthquakes and volcanic activity are more common; hence, volcanic basalt stones are plentiful in the Capernaum area.

3. The support for the roof would be wood beams or branches. These would be thatched together with reeds and mud daub. See R. T. France,

Controversies

The Gospel of Mark, New International Greek Testament Commentary (Grand Rapids, MI: Eerdmans, 2002), 123.

4. See France, *The Gospel of Mark*, 128; cf. Mark L. Strauss, *Mark*, Zondervan Exegetical Commentary on the New Testament (Grand Rapids, MI: Zondervan, 2014),123, 124.

5. See m. Shabbat 7:2.

6. See France, *The Gospel of Mark*, 145, 146.

7. See Robert A. Guelich, *Mark 1–8:26*, Word Biblical Commentary 34A (Dallas, TX: Word, 1989), 128.

8. This storytelling technique was the subject of my PhD dissertation. See Tom Shepherd, *Markan Sandwich Stories: Narration, Definition, and Function*, Andrews University Seminary Doctoral Dissertation Series 18 (Berrien Springs, MI: Andrews University Press, 1993).

9. The technical term for this ignorance in irony is *alazony*. The term comes from ancient Greek plays in which irony was depicted in some proud character who would take a great fall in the story. The audience could see what was coming, but the proud character, known as the *alazon*, could not see it coming.

4

Parables

You know how it happens. You are in a hurry to be somewhere—an important meeting, the store to buy something, or even church. You would not think of exceeding the speed limit (not you!), but you certainly want to go the speed limit. And then, just ahead, someone pulls out slowly in front of you, poking along at ten miles per hour slower than the speed limit. I seem to be a magnet for such people. Maybe you feel that way too.

In the same way, it is easy to hurry an interpretation of the Bible. People want a quick answer, a brief explanation, or a key point that they can take with them. After all, life is busy, and time is precious. But a brief answer can leave large gaps in one's understanding of the Word of God. That may be particularly true in the study of Jesus' parables. Many people see a parable as a simple story that illustrates a great truth, and all they must do is make the connection between the story's characters, their actions, and the truths Jesus is teaching, and voilà, you have the meaning of the parable—simple, direct, and clear.

But this hurried approach to parables can miss important

details, even within the parable itself. Slowing down to recognize these details adds depth to the points Jesus was making. After all, He often told the parable story and offered its interpretation. This is what we see in the story that dominates Mark 4—the parable of the sower.

The story of the sower and the soils

The English word *parable* comes from the Greek word *parabolē*. This word has a wider semantic domain, or set of meanings, in Greek than the English word *parable*. The Greek word can also mean "riddle, metaphor, analogy," or "proverb."[1] In the parable of the sower, the sower himself is not actually emphasized nor is he in the interpretation Jesus gives (Mark 4:3–9, 13–20). What is emphasized are the different soils that the seed falls on. Jesus describes four types of soil: a path, rocky ground, ground with weeds, and good ground. For His hearers, this type of description might call to mind how the Old Testament commonly referred to people by using metaphors of fields, plants, or trees (Psalms 1:3; 44:2; 72:16; Isaiah 5:1–7; Jeremiah 2:21; Ezekiel 19:10–14; Daniel 4).

Jesus tells the story of four soils, but He does not describe the field as a whole. Rather, He focuses attention on each type of soil by telling its story from beginning to end. Then He moves on to the next type of soil. This manner of storytelling places emphasis on the particular details of each soil and its outcome.

The first three stories—path, rocky ground, and ground with weeds—all end the same way: a failure to produce a crop. This type of pattern, known as a *multiple singularity* in storytelling (the repetition of the same action over and over), leads to the expectation that the final story will have the same pattern. When it does not, the final story becomes a contrasting punch line or conclusion that receives more emphasis by being different. It is something like saying, John went to the store on Monday, John went to the store on Tuesday, John went to the store on Wednesday, *but* on Thursday, John went to the ball game. In the parable, the final story's big harvest of thirtyfold, sixtyfold, and a hundredfold adds to the emphasis.

The number of words dedicated to the story of each soil varies. The greatest number of words is given to the rocky soil, followed by the good soil. This detail could simply be the result of what is necessary to explain the outcome for that specific soil. But this seems less likely in Mark 4, particularly with the rocky soil, since a certain amount of repetition occurs in the telling. Furthermore, we have already noted the emphasis on the good soil from its yield. One other feature of the good soil calls for comment. The good soil succeeds in exactly the places where the other soils fail. The seed that falls on the good soil grows up, whereas the seed on the path disappears. The seed on the good soil increases, whereas the seed on the rocky soil withers. The seed on the good soil yields fruit, whereas the seed on the weed-infested soil fails to yield grain. Thus, the good soil is the antithesis of the other soils.

In Jesus' interpretation of this parable (verses 13–20), He explains the meaning of each of the soils and why they failed to produce results or, in the case of the good soil, why it produced abundant results. Jesus devotes the most time to explaining the rocky ground and the ground with weeds in His unpacking of the parable's meaning. By placing the story details and their interpretations next to each other, we can better understand what stands in the way of a successful Christian life and witness.

Soil type	Story detail	Story meaning
Path	Birds devour	Satan takes away the Word
Rocky	No depth, scorched, and withered	Accept the Word with joy but give way when persecuted
Weeds	Weeds choke; no yield	Cares of the world, riches, and desires choke the Word; no yield
Good	Grows, increases, and yields	Hear the Word, accept it, and bear fruit

It is interesting to see how obstacles to a successful Christian life often stand in contrast to one another. For example, the seed that fell on the path represents listeners who are inattentive; they do not care about spiritual things. But the rocky-soil listeners are just the opposite. They accept the Word with joy, unlike the path listeners. However, they, too, fail in taking root because when persecution comes, their experience is exposed and they fall away. In contrast to the rocky-soil listeners, the weed-infested listeners do not fail because of the pressure of persecution. Instead, they fail because of the attractiveness of worldly affairs. The pull of the world's glitter and glamour prove to be more attractive than the straight message of the Word.

Finally, there is a sharp distinction between the failed listeners and the good-soil listeners. The good-soil listeners hear the Word, just like all the other listeners (note the use of "hear" in Mark 4:15, 16, 18, 20), but they accept the Word and bear fruit. They are not inattentive, shallow, or distracted. They are focused on the Word, and it bears fruit in their lives.

The problematic Mark 4:10–12

In the midst of telling the parable of the sower and its explanation, Jesus is asked by His disciples and "those around him . . . about the parables" (verse 10).[2] Jesus responds with a stark statement that "the secret of the kingdom of God" has been given to those now listening to Jesus—the disciples and "those around him"—but not to outsiders (verse 11). For the outsiders, everything is in parables (which may be better translated as "riddles" in this context).

Then Jesus paraphrases Isaiah 6:9, 10, saying this is

"so that

" 'they may indeed see but not perceive,
   and may indeed hear but not understand,
lest they should turn and be forgiven' " (Mark 4:12).

To many readers, this sounds as though Jesus tells parables to keep outsiders in the dark since if they really understood, they would repent and be forgiven. It is not hard to see how these words prove to be a stumbling block for some people.

A detailed explanation of these verses is beyond the space limits of this chapter.[3] However, we can summarize details that illustrate that Jesus was not trying to keep outsiders away. It was their prior choices concerning His mission that kept them on the outside.

The first clue to note for recognizing what Jesus is teaching in these verses appears in Mark 4:10. It states that when Jesus "was alone, those around him with the twelve asked him about the parables." Who were these other people? Why were they with Jesus when He was alone? We are not told their identities, but it is clear that they wanted additional insights on the parable He told the larger crowd before He moved to a more private location.

What this suggests is that the gift of receiving the "secret of the kingdom of God" revolves around the personal choice of an individual who has enough interest to seek it out. This is similar to what Jesus says in John 7:17: "If anyone's will is to do God's will, he will know whether the teaching is from God or whether I am speaking on my own authority."

Clue number two regarding the meaning of Mark 4:10–12 is that the perspective we are arguing for perfectly matches the details of the parable of the sower and its interpretation. Pathway hearers are uninterested in the Word of God and simply let Satan snatch it away. Rocky-ground hearers like what they hear but have not counted the cost of discipleship. Weedy-ground hearers are distracted by the glitter and glamour of the world, and the Word does not bear fruit in their lives. It is the good-ground hearers who persist in seeking out Jesus, letting the Word transform their lives, and energizing their mission to bear fruit.

But what about those challenging words in Mark 4:12—those who see but do not perceive, and those who hear but do not understand, lest they turn and be forgiven? Doesn't that sound like a hard Jesus who is uninterested in helping outsiders?

In Mark 4:12, Jesus is paraphrasing Isaiah 6:9, 10, as noted above. The context in Isaiah 6 is the call of Isaiah. He has a vision of the temple of God, and God Himself is arrayed in glorious apparel, seated on His throne. Angels call out to one another, "Holy, holy, holy is the LORD of hosts; / the whole earth is full of his glory!" (verse 3). The prophet is overwhelmed and exclaims, "Woe is me! For I am lost; for I am a man of unclean lips, and I dwell in the midst of a people of unclean lips; for my eyes have seen the King, the LORD of hosts!" (verse 5). But then an angel takes a coal from the altar and touches Isaiah's lips, telling him that his guilt is taken away.

This amazing picture of God's majesty and power is followed by His call, "Whom shall I send, and who will go for us?" (verse 8). Isaiah volunteers, and then he is given the message of rebuke in verses 9, 10. It seems odd that a prophet would be commissioned to harden people in unbelief. However, while the rest of Isaiah does rebuke wickedness (e.g., Isaiah 28–31), there is actually a great deal of comfort for God's people (cf. Isaiah 40–66).

What is likely occurring in Isaiah 6:9, 10 is hyperbole. God addresses the people in this way because they are already closed in their thinking. The people have already demonstrated their lack of interest in change (cf. Isaiah 5:1–7), so God speaks in hyperbolic, over-the-top language to shake them out of their stupor and turn their hearts back to Him.

The same type of wayward rejection of God's message is apparent in the Gospel of Mark. In Mark 3:22–30, the religious leaders claim that Jesus is possessed by the devil. One can hardly think of a stronger dismissal of His message. No one in their right mind would want to listen to the devil. This type of negative response to Jesus leads to the unpardonable sin—rejection of the pleadings of the Holy Spirit. If you call the Spirit of God a demon, you cut yourself off from receiving His appeal.

But the truth is that Jesus had no desire for the religious leaders to be lost. This fact is illustrated by the third clue regarding Jesus' teaching in Mark 4:10–12. Jesus is concerned over the religious leaders' rejection of His message. In Mark 3:1–6—the dispute over healing on the Sabbath—Jesus expresses ongoing grief at the hardness of the hearts of the leaders (verse 5). This response does not sound like someone who does not care about outsiders. Furthermore, in the parable of the vineyard (Mark 12:1–12), verse 12 specifically indicates that the leaders understood Jesus' parable. He did not tell the parable to keep them in the dark but rather to warn them of where their steps were headed.

Thus, like the vision in Isaiah 6, Jesus uses hyperbole in Mark 4:10–12 to draw attention to the leaders' attack on Him and their rejection of His message. In contrast, those who sincerely wanted to know the gospel received the message that Jesus brought.

These stories still speak to us today. They promise great light and hope to those who accept Jesus' message but give a strong warning to those who are inattentive or actively reject it.

---

1. See Mark L. Strauss, *Mark*, Zondervan Exegetical Commentary on the New Testament (Grand Rapids, MI: Zondervan, 2014), 179.

2. Note that it is "parables," not *parable*. They are not simply asking about the parable of the sower but about *all* the parables. Some readers stumble over this plural reference since the parable of the sower is apparently the first parable in Mark. But it is not. The term *parabolē* ("parable, riddle, metaphor") is used in Mark 3:23, which is followed by what some might call illustrations, but we might better say metaphors. Also, in Mark 4:2, we are told that Jesus taught "many things in parables." Thus, it is not an error for the plural term "parables" to be used in Mark 4:10. This indicates that the application of what Jesus will say extends beyond just the parable of the sower.

3. See the much fuller explanation in the Mark commentary of the Seventh-day Adventist International Bible Commentary (Nampa, ID: Pacific Press®, forthcoming) on this passage.

5

Miracles Around the Lake

Jesus spent most of His ministry in the northern Palestine region of Galilee. As we noted earlier, the Sea of Galilee is a small lake in comparison with many bodies of water in the world. It is only about thirteen miles long (twenty-one kilometers) and eight miles across (thirteen kilometers) at its widest point. However, it is the largest body of fresh water in Palestine. It is located in a depression, with mountains rising on both the east and the west—a feature that is conducive to storms descending quickly on the lake. It sits at 686 feet below sea level. It drains southward into the Jordan River, which flows down the Jordan Valley for sixty-five miles (105 kilometers), emptying into the Dead Sea, which sits at 1,410 feet below sea level and is the lowest land point in the world.

Mark 4 ends with Jesus in a boat on the Sea of Galilee, weathering a storm with His disciples. He calms the storm by simply speaking to the wind and waves, much to the amazement of His disciples. Chapter 6 closes with another scene on the lake. This time Jesus walks on the water to reach His frightened disciples. Between these two storm stories, Mark 5 and 6 present Jesus performing a variety of miracles and activities on the land adjoining the lake. We will focus on several of those stories in this chapter.

A demoniac at the Gadarenes

The storm on the lake that Jesus calms (Mark 4:35–41) is matched by the "storm" of a crazy, demon-possessed man meeting Jesus when He arrives in "the country of the Gadarenes" (Mark 5:1, NKJV). The eastern side of the lake was largely Gentile in population, explaining the large herd of pigs being tended nearby. The demon-possessed man's story is filled with uncleanness and defilement. He dwells in the tombs, which are places of death and ritual defilement (Numbers 19:14–16). Because the land was populated by Gentiles and their idols, the Old Testament designates the land as polluted (Jeremiah 2:23; Psalm 106:36–40). The huge herd of pigs added to the uncleanness of the occasion (Leviticus 11), and the possessed man, cut and bloodied, was also linked with defilement (Leviticus 15). To top things off, the demon possessing the man is called "unclean" (Mark 5:2).

With this totality of defilement, one might suspect that coming to such a place would defile an observant Jew. But that was not the case with Jesus. In Mark 1, Jesus encountered a leper seeking healing. Touching such a person was defiling (Leviticus 13; Numbers 5:1–4), but Jesus is not defiled by healing the leper. Instead, the leprosy leaves the man. Jesus' power is cleansing in nature, and when He arrives in the Gadarenes, He is as a cleansing agent for a defiled land.

The Evangelist paints a grim picture of the demon-possessed man's situation. He lived alone in tombs since he broke away from anyone who tried to constrain him. He demonstrated superhuman strength, breaking shackles that bound him. Night and day, he was crying out and cutting himself with stones on the mountains and in the tombs. Human help was impossible, and the demons controlled him. But then he met Jesus.

This encounter with Jesus is impressive for several reasons. The man runs up to Jesus and bows before Him. The term used to describe this bowing is *proskyneō*—the verb that typically means "to worship." It does not necessarily mean that here but may well represent a distinction between the man who senses that Jesus can help him and the demons who control his voice and produce a shouting confrontation with the Lord.

In Mark 5:7, the demons shout through the man, "What have you to do with me, Jesus, Son of the Most High God? I adjure you by God, do not torment me." Rather strangely, the verbs relating to the man shift back and forth between singular and plural, illustrating the dichotomy in his life between himself and the demons inside. The demons know who Jesus is and recognize His superior power. Almost humorously, they adjure Him in the name of God not to torment them. How could the devil's agents expect God to restrain Jesus from saving a demon-possessed man? The Greek term here for "adjure" is *horkizō*, which means "to implore" or "to make one swear." It was used in exorcism to put a demon under oath to come out of a person. This fact suggests that the demons may have been trying to cast Jesus out of their territory.

Jesus has a brief conversation with the demons. His first words are to tell them to come out of the man. These words are what called forth the plea not to torment them. Jesus asks the demons their name, and they respond, "Legion" (verse 9). A Roman legion consisted of six thousand soldiers, though the term here might not refer to an exact number but rather to the demons' claim that "we are many" (verse 9).

The demons plead with Jesus not to expel them from the territory. Where they would go is not stated, though the unclean land seems to be their logical dwelling place. They plead with Jesus to send them into the pigs, which is a fitting place for unclean spirits. Jesus agrees, and the pigs go wild, run down a steep bank, and drown in the sea.

The Gospel of Luke adds a detail that plays off the meaning of the sea. In Luke 8:31, the demons plead not to be sent into the "abyss." This is the same term used in the Greek Old Testament to refer to the chaos before God creates light on the first day (Genesis 1:2). It is also used to refer to the place Satan is confined during the millennium (Revelation 20:2, 3). After entering the pigs, the demons in Mark 5 end up in the water of the lake—another abyss!

The aftermath of the healing is again striking. The pig herders go to their village and report what has happened. People are amazed to find the demon-possessed man sitting, clothed, and in his right mind. This frightens them, and they beg Jesus to leave. As Jesus is getting into the boat, the healed man begs to go with Him. Jesus refuses and sends the man back into the community, charging him to tell what God has done for him.

In this story, three individuals or groups beg Jesus for something. The demons beg not to be expelled from the country, the townspeople beg Jesus to leave, and the healed man begs to be with Jesus. Jesus allows the first two but not the third. What are we to make of this? Here are three things to consider. First, Jesus has power over demons; they are no match for Him. Second, Jesus does not stay where He is not wanted. And finally, when you have experienced God's grace, tell others about it.

Jairus and the woman with the hemorrhage

Mark 5:21–43 immediately follows the story of the healing of the Gadarene demoniac. The story of Jarius and the woman with the hemorrhage is one of the Markan sandwich stories introduced in chapter 3. In this type of story, two parallel characters do opposite actions, or two opposite characters do parallel actions. In this case, we have two opposite characters who do parallel actions with ironic results. Both Jairus and the woman come to Jesus for help. The synagogue ruler brings an acute case, with his daughter at the point of death; and the woman comes with a chronic case, as she's been bleeding for twelve years. Strangely, Jesus heals the chronic case first, but while He is tending to the woman with the hemorrhage, the twelve-year-old girl dies.

There are numerous parallels between Jairus and the bleeding woman, as the following table illustrates:

Jairus	Woman
Male	Female
Synagogue ruler	Largely excluded from religious life
Comes in front of Jesus	Comes from behind Jesus
Sees Jesus	Hears about Jesus
Starts in public, ends in private	Starts in private, ends in public
Healed last	Healed first
Acute case	Chronic case
Twelve-year-old daughter	Twelve years of suffering

These parallels and contrasts play into the drama of the story. Jesus goes with Jairus to his house without any comment. His action in going speaks volumes about His willingness to help anyone in need, even a typical enemy.

The public approach of Jairus and his acute need stands in sharp contrast to the story of the woman. Her story interrupts Jairus's story, which is typical of sandwich stories, and is introduced by a long litany of her trouble. In English, her backstory is usually presented in several sentences, but in Greek, it is one long sentence. In fact, it is one long subordinate clause leading up to the central verb of the sentence—"to touch" Jesus' clothes. Her troubles are distilled into a single touch. The following sentence gives the reason for this laser focus: "For she said, 'If I touch even his garments, I will be made well' " (verse 28). The evangelist stresses her singular desire by the use of the imperfect tense (actions in the past that occurred repeatedly) in describing her statement. It can well be translated, "For she kept on saying . . ."

When she touches Jesus, her flow of blood immediately stops, and she knows she is well (verse 29). We can imagine that physiologically, before that touch, her blood hemoglobin has dropped quite low, perhaps down to seven or eight grams per deciliter (g/dL) or lower. With the miracle, her hemoglobin is immediately at a normal level (12–16 g/dL for women). Her vascular system also needs immediate healing to handle the increased load. No doubt she instantly feels exhilaratingly well and healthy. She may shift backward and take a deep breath with the feeling of perfect health for the first time in twelve years.

But Jesus stops, turns, and asks, "Who touched my garments?" (verse 30). It is an odd question in the midst of the pressing crowd. But there is a difference between the touch of faith and the casual touch of the throng. Well aware of Jesus' persistence, the woman knows she cannot remain hidden. Mark notes that she comes forward with "fear and trembling" (verse 32). But why the fear? She had not asked Jesus to heal her. Maybe she is concerned that she is defiled by the bleeding. Maybe she fears that He is angry, even to the point of anxiety that He might take the healing back. In any case, she tells her entire story, and Jesus blesses her with the benediction of peace.

But for Jairus, it is a terrible moment. While Jesus healed the woman, his daughter died. What tragic words for any father to hear: "Your daughter is dead. Why trouble the Teacher any further?" (verse 35). Jesus, overhearing this exchange, quickly turns His steps to Jairus's house. The mourners are already present, making it easy to identify Jairus's home. The commotion jars Jesus. He asks, "Why are you making a commotion and weeping? The child is not dead but sleeping" (verse 39). Like the strange question about someone touching His clothes in a crowd, this statement at the house of Jairus strikes the listeners as odd, even comical. They laugh at Him, and He throws them out.

In Jesus' day, the phrase "fall asleep" was a euphemism for dying, similar to our saying that a person has "passed away." But Jesus could not be using the terminology in that way since it would mean something like saying, "She is not dead; she has passed away." No wonder the laughter. But Jesus is using the term in a different way. His intent is more than the simple declaration He has made, just as His question about who had touched His clothes was more than a query about a chance touch of His person. In this case, He speaks of death as a sleep because He is able to raise the dead, just as we would awaken someone by touching or shaking that person.

Jesus takes the little girl's hand and says in Aramaic, "*Talitha koum!*" (verse 41, NIV). Mark interprets this as "Little girl, I say to you, arise" (verse 41). *Talitha* is actually the Aramaic word for "lamb." It was likely a term of endearment used in the home, just as people today will call a child "sweetheart" or some similar term. Jesus tells Jairus and his wife not to make the miracle known. How they would keep such an event secret when so many people had witnessed the child's death is not explained. This detail plays into the revelation-secrecy motif of the Gospel of Mark, in which Jesus' identity as the Messiah cannot really be hidden; the truth will come out.

A mission begun; a mission silenced

Mark 6 contains the third sandwich story of the Gospel of Mark: Jesus sending the twelve disciples on a mission, placed around the tragic beheading of John the Baptist. Most of the passage is consumed with the dramatic and grotesque story of John's beheading by Herod. This Herod was one of the sons of Herod the Great. His full name was Herod Antipas. He ruled Galilee and Perea from the death of his father in 4 BC through AD 39, when he was deposed by the emperor Caligula.[1]

His contact with John the Baptist occurred after John rebuked him for marrying Herodias, his brother Philip's wife. In modern democracies, citizens have the freedom to criticize leaders without too much fear of reprisal. It was not so in the ancient world and is not even so in some of today's traditional or closed societies. At the time, to criticize a leader was to invite punishment. Herod had John jailed, possibly at the fortress of Machaerus, which sits on the eastern side of the Dead Sea.[2]

The story of John's beheading revolves around the ambivalence of Herod toward the prophet and Herodias's hatred of John. Herodias tricks the king by sending her daughter to a banquet to dance for him and his guests. When the king promises to give her what she wants most, she surprises and shocks him by asking for the head of John the Baptist on a platter. Not wanting to go back on his word, the king relents when no one at the party objects.

The Baptist's death precedes and forecasts the death of Jesus. Just like John, Jesus will be arrested and put to death. Some had reported that John the Baptist was raised from the dead (Mark 6:14), and Jesus will rise from the dead. Thus, the Baptist is the forerunner of Christ in more ways than one. The end of the Baptist's ministry stands in contrast to the successful mission of the disciples. Ironically, as John's voice is silenced, the disciples share the gospel message.

1. See Mark L. Strauss, *Mark*, Zondervan Exegetical Commentary on the New Testament (Grand Rapids, MI: Zondervan, 2014), 261; Flavius Josephus, *Antiquities of the Jews* 18.7.1–2; Flavius Josephus, *Jewish War* 2.9.6.

2. Strauss, *Mark*, 264; Josephus, *Antiquities of the Jews* 18.5.2.

6

Inside Out

Washing one's hands is such a common activity that one might wonder who would ever oppose it. So, it may come as a surprise that Jesus seems to do just that at the beginning of Mark 7. But that would be to misunderstand the context in which Jesus opposes the Pharisees' tradition of handwashing.

In Jesus' day, a great number of Jews in Palestine were concerned with ritual purity. We know this from the number of ritual baths (called *mikvah*) and stone water jars used to hold water for purification (John 2:6). These jars have been discovered throughout Palestine from the time of Jesus.[1] This idea of purity was not linked to the question of hygiene, but rather, it was tied to ritual purity.

In Mark 7:4, the Evangelist notes that the Jews of Jesus' day would wash things when they came from the market-place. The reason for this washing was that one could not know whether the purchased food had come in contact with defiled items or persons.[2] This was all in keeping with the oral traditions that the Pharisees believed were passed down from Moses.[3] They took these traditions to be authoritative and binding, and they became the basis of the conflict with Jesus.

Mark notes that some of Jesus' disciples ate with unwashed hands. Evidently, some followed the practices of the Pharisees in ritual washing, while others did not. From this datum, it seems that Jesus did not make it a matter of discussion before this dispute. He neither affirmed nor rejected the disciples' practices in this regard. But now that the Pharisees criticize His disciples' practices—or more accurately, their lack of practice—the Lord responds to the Pharisaic teaching.

The Old Testament only requires the priests to do ritual washing before offering sacrifices or entering the sanctuary (Exodus 30:17–21). Either the Pharisees were extending the ritual washings to all Jews (perhaps as a kind of "priesthood of all believers"), or they may have been adapting Greco-Roman meal customs within a Jewish setting.[4] Regardless, they criticized Jesus' disciples and, by proxy, Jesus Himself.

Traditions of men or the commandments of God?

Jesus launches into a rather sharp critique of the Pharisaic plan. Rather than respond to the Pharisees' question, He criticizes them, using the words of Isaiah (Isaiah 29:13):

> " 'This people honors me with their lips,
>   but their heart is far from me;
>   in vain do they worship me,
>   teaching as doctrines the commandments of men' "
>   (Mark 7:6, 7).

Jesus calls the Pharisees hypocrites. In Greek, the term *hypokritēs* means "interpreter, actor, pretender." This term was used to refer to actors wearing masks in a play. They pretended to be a person other than themselves. Jesus says that the Pharisees were perpetrating a serious deception: they claimed to be following God, but their rules made it possible to escape following the commandments of God.

The example Jesus used is a rule called *corban*. The Greek term is *korban*, which means "gift." It is derived from the Hebrew term *qorban*, which refers to an offering dedicated to God. A vow made in this manner was irrevocable (Deuteronomy 23:21–23). Jesus is not speaking against making vows to God. What He attacks is using this idea of a vowed gift as a means of not helping one's father or mother materially. If a son with means said to his parents, "Anything you would receive from me is *korban*," the son would be able to keep the "gift" for his own use and not help his parent because the "gift" would be dedicated to God and thus unusable by the parent.

Such pious hypocrisy was particularly odious to Jesus, and He rebukes it strongly in Mark 7. He compares it to the command to honor one's father and mother, which is part of the Decalogue. Some people today might think that honoring one's parents means respecting them and saying good things about them. It does include that, but the commandment also has in mind caring for one's parents in their old age. Here is honor put in practical terms.

Inside out

Having rebuked the Pharisees for their practices, Jesus calls the crowd together and presents a pithy statement that counters the hypocrisy of the leaders: "There is nothing outside a person that by going into him can defile him, but the things that come out of a person are what defile him" (Mark 7:15). The word translated as "defile" here is the verb *koinoō*, "to defile, make common." It is the verbal equivalent of the adjective *koinos* ("common, ordinary, defiled"), which is used in Mark 7:2 in reference to the disciples eating with "defiled" hands, which Mark interprets as unwashed.

In His pithy statement, Jesus turns the Pharisaic rule on its head. Instead of something from outside the person ritually defiling that person, Jesus indicates that what really defiles is that which comes from the inside and goes out. Many people have the idea that what Jesus is doing here is abolishing the food laws regarding unclean meats (Leviticus 11; Deuteronomy 14). But this is to misunderstand the passage and what Jesus is teaching.

First, we present three reasons why the common understanding of abolishing the food laws concerning unclean meats is *not* what Jesus was teaching. Reason number one is that in the first half of the passage (Mark 7:1–13), Jesus defends Moses and the Law. If, in the second half of the passage (verses 14–23), He does away with part of the Old Testament Law, He undermines His own argument in defense of Moses and the Law. Reason number two is that purity scholars and historical Jesus scholars doubt that in the first century, Jesus could actually have taught that the food laws were done away with in the setting of Palestinian Judaism.[5] It would not have been acceptable. And reason number three, Mark uses specialized vocabulary in Mark 7:1–23 that he does not use elsewhere in his Gospel—*koinos*, "defiled," and *koinoō*, "to defile." The use of these terms suggests the specialized sense of Jesus' argument.

So what is Jesus saying? As it turns out, the disciples are unclear on Jesus' meaning, so in the manner typical of the Gospel of Mark, He explains the meaning to them. First, He gives a physiology lesson. Food enters the body, goes into the stomach, and then out into the latrine.[6] It does not have a permanent residence in the person. Food does not enter the heart, meaning the intellectual and spiritual center of a person. It just passes through the digestive system.

But the heart is a different matter. Jesus refers to evils that come from the heart—the intellectual and spiritual center of the person. The Lord enumerates thirteen evils that come from inside. He begins with an internal heart matter—evil thoughts. Whereas the religious leaders stressed the importance of outward cleansing, Jesus refers to inward evil that defiles. Evil thoughts lead to evil deeds.

The evil deeds enumerated fall into two groups: the first six are all in the plural in Greek, while the last six are in the singular. The plural items are sexually immoral actions, thefts, murders, acts of adultery, covetous acts, and acts of wickedness. The singular items in the list are deceit, sensuality, envy, slander, pride, and foolishness.

The thirteen items focus attention on human relationships. Strikingly, all six of the Ten Commandments that deal with human relationships are referenced in this passage:

- Honor to parents: fifth commandment (Mark 7:10)
- Murder: sixth commandment (verse 21)
- Adultery: seventh commandment (verse 21)
- Theft: eighth commandment (verse 21)
- Deceit: ninth commandment (verse 22)
- Covetousness: tenth commandment (verse 22)

The first four commandments of the Decalogue deal with our relationship with God, particularly the question of worship. Jesus quotes from Isaiah 29:13, noting that the religious leaders worship God in vain, "teaching as doctrines the commandments of men" (Mark 7:6). Consequently, throughout the entire passage of Mark 7:1–23, Jesus stands and defends the Law of God—the principles enshrined in the Ten Commandments. These details counter those who think Jesus is doing away with a teaching of the Law. Instead, He supports the Law.

The challenge of Mark 7:19

The place most commentators point to in support of their view that Jesus did away with the food laws reads like this in the ESV: "And he said to them, 'Then are you also without understanding? Do you not see that whatever goes into a person from outside cannot defile him, since it enters not his heart but his stomach, and is expelled?' (Thus he declared all foods clean)" (verses 18, 19). It is the last phrase, in parentheses, that is the source of this viewpoint. What does it mean?

First of all, the phrase in Greek is much more concise than what we find in most translations. Literally translated, verse 19 reads, "Because it does not enter into his heart but into the stomach, and goes out into the latrine, cleansing all the foods." The last phrase—"cleansing all the foods"—is what the ESV translates as "Thus he declared all foods clean." We can see that the ESV and most translations demonstrate a bias in translating the phrase in that way. This does not mean that their translation is incorrect, just that it is interpretive to a certain extent.

What should be kept in mind is the context in which these words are placed. There is no reference in the passage to the foods listed in Leviticus 11 and Deuteronomy 14. They would never have appeared on a table in a Jewish home. What is being discussed is ritual purity regulations—the touch contamination that had been developed in the intertestamental period. Jesus rejected those regulations since they had no basis in the Old Testament. Declaring all foods clean would mean that they could not transmit impurity.

This action by Jesus had far-reaching implications. It allowed Jews to eat with Gentiles, which is a topic that comes up in Acts 10 and 11 and Galatians 2. It did take some time for believers to understand and practice what Jesus was teaching, but His action opened the door for the inclusion of Gentiles and fellowship between Jews and Gentiles, which was an extremely important issue in the ancient church.

Jesus' teaching has implications for us today as well. God accepts people from all levels of society, all races, and all backgrounds. Prejudice and separation between peoples are rejected and done away with by Jesus' simple statement that it is not what goes in that defiles but what comes out. He stands in solidarity with the Old Testament teaching that God loves people of all races and nationalities.

A persistent woman finds help at Jesus' table

Immediately following the discussion of what defiles is the story that addresses the inclusion of Gentiles in the community of faith. However, it is a most unusual story. It is the only story in the Gospels where someone argues with Jesus and wins. It is the only story where Jesus departs Palestine during His ministry. It is also the only time that Jesus as much as called a person a dog. The short story, filled with twists and turns, is about a Syrophoenician woman and her demon-possessed daughter (Mark 7:24–30).

As the story begins, it seems that Jesus is seeking a retreat from the bustle of His ministry. He goes to the region of Tyre and Sidon, enters a house, and wants no one to know about it. But a Syrophoenician woman found His retreat and sought Him out. Falling at His feet, she implored Jesus to cast the demon out of her daughter.

Typically, in the Gospels, when people make this type of request, Jesus responds by expelling the demon. In fact, throughout the four Gospels, anyone who comes to Jesus for help receives it. Consequently, it is quite shocking that Jesus rebuffs the woman with the words, "Let the children be fed first, for it is not right to take the children's bread and throw it to the dogs" (verse 27).

Some years ago, I taught World Religions at Union College in Lincoln, Nebraska. I invited guest lecturers of different religions to share with the class what was precious to them about their faith. Students could ask questions afterward. One student boldly asked a rabbi why he did not believe in Jesus.

The rabbi responded that he did not believe in Jesus because He called a woman a dog. So it is not hard to see the strong character of Jesus' response. But several points in the story demonstrate that Jesus was actually encouraging the woman to press her request.

First, the word *dog* in this story is a diminutive. It does not mean "puppies" in context but rather dogs that were allowed in the house. It is true that Jesus calls the woman a dog—but a house dog. Not only that, the woman is in a house with Jesus and is at His feet, much like house dogs would be in their masters' homes. The woman, no doubt, grasps that point when she presses her request.

Second, in Mark 7:27, Jesus says, "Let the children be fed *first* . . ." He is clearly referring to the Jews in contrast to the Gentiles. But if there is a *first*, it implies there will also be a *second*. The woman undoubtedly grasps this as well. Lest we think it strange that the Jews would be first in line, so to speak, to hear the gospel message, Paul states in Romans 1:16: "For I am not ashamed of the gospel, for it is the power of God for salvation to everyone who believes, *to the Jew first* and also to the Greek" (emphasis added). As God's chosen people, the Jews would receive the call to follow the Messiah first. But this did not exclude the Gentiles. They, too, would receive the call.

The woman, picking up on these cues, gives a bold, thoughtful response to Jesus: "Lord, . . . even the dogs under the table eat the children's crumbs" (Mark 7:28, NIV).[7] She will accept the moniker *dog* to obtain her request for her daughter. She also refers to the miracle she seeks as simply a crumb from the table. In this way, she exalts the power of Jesus—the miracle would be as small as a crumb for Him to perform—while at the same time suggesting that what she asks for is not a grand sacrifice of resources reserved for the Jews. It is just a "crumb" falling from the table. Jesus is struck by her reply and grants her request.

But still, why call her a dog? Wasn't that offensive? It was, both then and now. With all we know about Jesus, it seems odd that He would use this term. Ellen White, in *The Desire of Ages*, pulls aside the curtain to explain His intention. Speaking of the Matthean telling of the story, where Jesus does not respond immediately to the woman, she notes: "Christ did not immediately reply to the woman's request. He received this representative of a despised race as the Jews would have done. In this He designed that His disciples should be impressed with the cold and heartless manner in which the Jews would treat such a case, as evinced by His reception of the woman, and the compassionate manner in which He would have them deal with such distress, as manifested by His subsequent granting of her petition."[8]

Ellen White's remarks show that the parables and miracles of Jesus taught many lessons to the children of God. Jesus' actions and words were a lesson book on how to act and how *not* to act in relation to the needs of those around us.

---

1. See Adela Yarbro Collins, *Mark*, Hermeneia (Minneapolis, MN: Fortress, 2007), 345–347; Joel Marcus, *Mark 1–8*, Anchor Bible 27 (New York: Doubleday, 2000), 440, 441. Jars made from clay had to be broken if they became defiled, hence the value of stone jars (cf. Leviticus 6:28; 11:33; 15:12).

2. See Mark L. Strauss, *Mark*, Zondervan Exegetical Commentary on the New Testament (Grand Rapids, MI: Zondervan, 2014), 298–300.

3. See m. Avot 1.1; Flavius Josephus, *Antiquities of the Jews* 13.10.6; Collins, *Mark*, 345–349; Strauss, *Mark*, 298, 299.

4. See Collins, *Mark*, 344, 345; Jacob Neusner, *A History of the Mishnaic Law of Purities*, vol. 19 (Leiden, Netherlands: Brill, 1976), 103; Hannah K. Harrington, *The Impurity Systems of Qumran and the Rabbis: Biblical Foundations*, Society of Biblical Literature Dissertation Studies 143 (Atlanta, GA: Scholars Press, 1993), 280, 281. See also Yair Fursten-

berg, "Defilement Penetrating the Body: A New Understanding of Contamination in Mark 7.15," *New Testament Studies* 54, no. 2 (2008): 176–200. For rabbinic discussions in the Mishnah, see m. Tahorot and m. Yadayim.

5. See Thomas Kazen, *Jesus and Purity* Halakhah*: Was Jesus Indifferent to Impurity?*, Coniectanea Biblica: New Testament Series 38 (Stockholm, Sweden: Almqvist & Wiksell, 2002); E. P. Sanders, *Jesus and Judaism* (Philadelphia: Fortress, 1985); E. P. Sanders, *The Historical Figure of Jesus* (London: Allen Lane, 1993); Jacob Neusner, *Purity in Rabbinic Judaism: A Systematic Account*, South Florida Studies in the History of Judaism 95 (Atlanta, GA: Scholars Press, 1994).

6. Some translations soften verse 19 by saying, "Since it enters not his heart but his stomach, and is expelled" (ESV). But in Greek, the phrase is "goes out into the latrine."

7. Verse 28 in the ESV has the reply as "Yes, Lord; yet even the dogs under the table eat the children's crumbs." There is a textual variant here, with some manuscripts having "Yes, Lord," and others simply using "Lord," which gives a little more pushback in its feel. The word "yet" in the ESV does not appear in the Greek text.

8. Ellen G. White, *The Desire of Ages* (Mountain View, CA: Pacific Press®, 1940), 400.

7

Teaching Disciples, Part 1

All of us have transition points in our lives—leaving home for the first time, graduating from school, getting that first job, getting married, the birth of a child, a promotion, and the death of a loved one. These moments are memorable because they represent a shift in who we are and our understanding of life. We celebrate them when they represent hope and progress. We mourn them when they represent loss.

The Gospel of Mark is fairly evenly divided into two main sections: chapters 1–8 and chapters 8–16. Its turning point occurs in chapter 8, shifting from an emphasis on who Jesus is to a focus on where He is going. This transition was not an easy one for the disciples to process because it did not meet their expectations. Jesus was going to Calvary—a destination they never dreamed would be appropriate for Him.

Opening their eyes

The transition to the second half of the Gospel of Mark is introduced in an unusual way. It relates a story unique to Mark: the story of the healing of a blind man. Of course, Jesus often healed the blind in His ministry—Bartimaeus

(Mark 10:46–52), a man born blind (John 9), and two blind men (Matthew 20:29–34), to name a few. What is unusual here is that He does not completely heal the blindness on the first attempt. Rather, when He heals the man, He asks him what he sees. The man responds that he sees men walking about, but they look like trees. Jesus touches the man's eyes again, and then he sees clearly. What is going on here? It seems that this is an acted parable that illustrates the process of the disciples coming to understand better Jesus' mission and their own discipleship.

Moving on, Mark 8:22–10:52 forms a section of the Gospel focused on teaching the disciples about discipleship. It follows a rather organized pattern over these three chapters.

First, Jesus predicts His death and then follows with instruction for His disciples. This pattern appears three times with the predictions of His death (Mark 8:31; 9:31; 10:33, 34). In each case, Jesus follows His declaration with discipleship lessons. In Mark 8:34–9:1, He talks about the cost of discipleship. In Mark 9:33–50, He explains true greatness and cooperation with those who work for Jesus and warns about temptations to sin. In Mark 10:35–45, He responds to a request from James and John by teaching them about service to others as true greatness.

Surrounding this entire section are the two healings of blind men: the blind man healed with two touches in Mark 8:22–26 and the healing of blind Bartimaeus in Mark 10:46–52. The healing of the first blind man illustrates how the disciples are learning, little by little, just who Jesus is and what it means to follow Him. The healing of Bartimaeus illustrates the value of following Jesus after one has received spiritual sight.

The cost of discipleship
From the beginning, the Gospel of Mark makes it clear that

Jesus is the Messiah, the Son of God (Mark 1:1). However, the characters in the Gospel account, other than the demon-possessed people, do not recognize who He is. This fact gives us insights that the characters in the first half of the Gospel did not have. Our vantage point helps us to see what is taking place in the narrative and how the disciples progress toward a deeper understanding of who Jesus is.

But in Mark 8:27–30, the curtain is drawn aside when Jesus solemnly asks, "Who do people say that I am?" (verse 27). The disciples respond with some of the people's mistaken views of Jesus (cf. Mark 6:14–16). But then Jesus continues with the true question of discipleship: "But who do you say that I am?" It is Peter who responds with the clarion confession, "You are the Christ" (verse 29). We might think that at this point, Jesus would say, "That is right! Spread the news!" But instead, He tells His disciples to keep that knowledge to themselves. This command may seem baffling to us in the twenty-first century, but in the first century, claiming to be a messiah had political overtones that were dangerous for the person making the claim. This explains Jesus' command on a historical level. To make an open proclamation of this truth would have shortened His ministry.

But on a theological level, the call for secrecy has a different focus. Throughout Mark, we see revelation and secrecy side by side (cf. Mark 5:21–43 where Jairus and the woman with a hemorrhage illustrate revelation and secrecy: he starts in public but ends in secrecy; she starts in secrecy and tells all before the crowd). Here in Mark 8, it is no different. Jesus has just been revealed and confessed as the Messiah, but it must be kept secret for the time being. As the Gospel of Mark progresses, the truth emerges, along with the disciples' responsibility to proclaim the good news about their risen Lord.

After Peter confesses that Jesus is the Messiah, Jesus begins to open before His disciples just where He is headed—to a Roman cross. This is not what the disciples wanted to hear. Peter goes so far as to rebuke Jesus, using the same Greek word Jesus used when referring to the secrecy (*epitimaō*, "to rebuke, warn, or censure"). In His response to Peter, Jesus *warned* the disciples not to tell who He was, and Peter *warned* Jesus not to go down the path of suffering. This led to a sharp rebuke from Jesus, calling Peter "Satan" for suggesting something that was not in accordance with the will of God (verse 33).

After this exchange, Jesus unfolds to His disciples and the others with them what is involved in being His disciple. It is total self-denial, taking up the cross, and following Him. What is surprising, however, is the way in which Jesus supports His call to discipleship. In Mark 8:35–38, He points out the *value* of being a disciple—saving one's life by losing it, exchanging death for eternal life, and being unashamed when Jesus returns. In this light, self-denial is the path that brings true treasure and makes sense of what people typically think of as foolishly throwing away worldly gain.

The mountain and the multitude

The story of the Transfiguration and the encounter with the demon-possessed boy follows immediately after Peter's confession and Jesus' explanation of the cost of discipleship. In Mark 9:1, Jesus refers to some present "who will not taste death until they see the kingdom of God after it has come with power." This statement troubles some people because they think it suggests that first-century Christians expected Jesus to return in their day and that even Jesus Himself had that expectation.

Two details in Mark 9:1 point in a different direction. First, Jesus states that *some* standing there would see the kingdom come in power. The New Testament clearly teaches that *everyone* will see Jesus when He returns (Matthew 24; Mark 13; Luke 21; 1 Thessalonians 4:13–18; Revelation 1:7). Thus, *some* seeing it now suggests that this is a preview of that great and glorious day of His return.

Second, Jesus clearly states that the *some* who will see the kingdom coming in glory will later die: they "will not taste death *until* they see the kingdom of God having come in power" (Mark 9:1, LSB; emphasis added). They will *see* the kingdom in power, not *enter* it. And after that, they will die. Clearly, at the second coming of Jesus, the saints will no longer die (1 Thessalonians 4:13–18; 1 Corinthians 15). Hence, seeing "the kingdom having come in power" must be a preview of the great day when our Lord will return in glory. The story of the Transfiguration that follows in Mark 9:2–13 exactly fulfills this prediction and thus is what Jesus is talking about.

Exactly where the Transfiguration takes place is not specified. Two mountains that are often mentioned as possible sites are Mount Hermon, the tallest mountain near Caesarea Philippi, where Peter's confession occurs; and Mount Tabor, further to the south near the Valley of Jezreel. Since the mountain is unnamed in the text, we cannot know whether either of these mountains was the location of the Transfiguration. What is important is what happened on the mountain.

At the Transfiguration, Jesus is glorified and affirmed by God the Father. He meets with Elijah and Moses. Elijah never died before translation to heaven (2 Kings 2), and Moses served God, died, and was raised to life (Jude 9). These two heavenly visitants talk with Jesus on the mountain. Mark does not indicate what they say, but the Gospel of Luke states that they discuss His "departure" (Greek *exodos*), which will be accomplished in Jerusalem (Luke 9:31). During their time on earth, Moses and Elijah saw apostasy, sin, and failure, and they encourage Jesus as He faces His great sacrifice on the cross. His ordeal will be worth the experience of seeing souls redeemed in the kingdom (cf. Hebrews 12:2).

Three disciples—Peter, James, and John—witness the Transfiguration. It is an unforgettable experience. Peter suggests making three tents: one for Jesus, one for Moses, and one for Elijah. But then a cloud overshadows them, and the voice of God declares, "This is my beloved Son; listen to him" (Mark 9:7). This scene is reminiscent of God descending on Mount Sinai and proclaiming the Ten Commandments. It is a *theophany*—an appearance of God.

Theophanies in Scripture have five common characteristics: (1) the appearance of glory, (2) human fear, (3) the words "Do not fear," (4) a revelation from God, and (5) a human response. Most of these characteristics appear in this scene. The glory is Jesus' appearance and the cloud (verses 3, 7). The human fear is noted in verse 6. The revelation is God's proclamation that Jesus is His beloved Son and the disciples should listen to Him (verse 7). The human response is Peter's proposal to put up three tents (verse 5) and the discussion the disciples have with Jesus as they descend the mountain (verses 9–13).

The significance of the Transfiguration is its affirmation of Jesus as the Son of God. It confirms the disciples' faith in Jesus as the Crucifixion approaches. The reader knows this from the beginning of the Gospel (1:1), but it is important for the three disciples to recognize Jesus' identity to help them weather the storm of the Passion. Jesus deliberately seeks to prepare them for the cross with references to His death and resurrection and the demise of John the Baptist, the forerunner (verses 9, 12, 13).

At the base of the mountain, the scene is quite different from the Transfiguration. Jesus encounters a demon-possessed boy and his father. To their embarrassment, the nine disciples who had stayed behind at the base of the mountain could not cast out the demon. Jesus responds by bemoaning the unbelief of the people and even His own disciples.

Encountering unbelief after the mountaintop experience is not unlike Moses coming down from Mount Sinai with Joshua and encountering the Israelites worshiping the golden calf (Exodus 32:15–20). Like Moses, Jesus will overcome the evil at the foot of the mountain.

The boy that Jesus encounters is possessed by an unclean spirit. In Mark 9:18, six specific terms are used to describe the situation of the boy. The spirit (1) *seizes* the boy and (2) *throws* him *down*. The boy (3) *foams at the mouth*, (4) *grinds* his (5) *teeth*, and (6) *becomes rigid*. To those in the medical field, this likely sounds like the symptoms of epilepsy, but the Gospels attribute the boy's condition to demon possession. This is not to say that the Gospel writers were mistaken, attributing a neurological disorder to spiritual forces. The demonic possession may simply have mirrored in many ways what is known today as epilepsy. Furthermore, we should not go to the opposite extreme and call epilepsy and other disorders demon possession. The two are distinct in origin.[1]

An interesting aspect of this story is the attitude of the boy's father. He is overwhelmed by the disciples' failure to heal his son. When he meets Jesus, his faltering hope gives way to his plea, "But if you can do anything, have compassion on us and help us" (verse 22). Jesus retorts, " 'If you can'! All things are possible for one who believes" (verse 23). It is a sudden lightning-bolt revelation to the father that the problem is not simply his son's condition but his own faltering faith. He responds by casting himself on the Savior's mercy: "I believe; help my unbelief!" (verse 24). Jesus then heals the boy.

This story has important lessons. Our place in ministry is not simply to be with Jesus on the mountaintop of communion with God; it is also down in the valley with real people suffering real problems. Our calling is not simply to share the gospel message but also to live it out by practicing the love and mercy of God. Some people may have weak faith, but when we help them, it increases their faith.

The healthy man in hell

At the close of chapter 9, Jesus touches on two concepts that trouble people (verses 42–50). One is the idea of cutting off a hand or foot or plucking out an eye if it causes a person to sin. Should this command be taken literally? The other is the issue of what appears to be an eternally burning hell "where their worm does not die and the fire is not quenched" (verse 48, quoting Isaiah 66:24).

These two "problem texts" are an example of Jesus using hyperbole and comedy to make a point.[2] Jesus is not teaching self-mutilation. This was rejected in Judaism (Deuteronomy 14:1; 1 Kings 18:28).[3] Instead, He is illustrating that we should prefer to lose a hand, a foot, or an eye rather than commit a sin. Sin is serious business, and we should avoid it.

The comedy appears in a continuation of Jesus' example of drastic "surgery" by speaking of lame, blind, and disfigured people entering heaven because they "cut away" sin from their lives, while the healthy people with both eyes, both hands, and both feet go to hell. Again, it is not a literal picture but a comedic expression of the tragedy of clinging to sin. It will ruin our lives. It is far better to lose a limb or an eye than to cling to sin.

How do we know this is not a literal picture? Because those who enter the heavenly kingdom will be whole and healthy, not lame, blind, or disfigured (1 Corinthians 15). The hyperbole and comedy help us to understand that Jesus is making a point about the importance of abandoning sin; He is not recommending self-mutilation.

1. See the helpful discussion in R. T. France, *The Gospel of Mark*, New International Greek Testament Commentary (Grand Rapids, MI: Eerdmans, 2002), 362, 363. For a discussion of epilepsy and its treatment, see Mary J. England et al., eds., *Epilepsy Across the Spectrum: Promoting Health and Understanding* (Washington, DC: National Academies Press, 2012), https://nap.nationalacademies.org/catalog/13379/epilepsy-across-the-spectrum-promoting-health-and-understanding.

2. I sometimes ask my students how many problem texts there are in the Bible. It is a trick question. There are no problem texts in the Bible. The text is not the problem. It is our understanding of the text that is the problem.

3. See Mark L. Strauss, *Mark*, Zondervan Exegetical Commentary on the New Testament (Grand Rapids, MI: Zondervan, 2014), 413, 414.

8

Teaching Disciples, Part 2

Becoming a follower of Jesus is the decision of a moment but the work of a lifetime. Too often, we focus most of our attention on the beginning of the journey. It is joyous to see someone make a decision and seal it before a congregation in baptism, but the fostering of that decision in daily living is just as important. Training the young and old in what it means to follow Jesus helps them to live out their decision before others.

Crucial to growing disciples, especially young ones, are stable Christian homes, healthy church congregations, and Christian schools. These three institutions form a triad of purposeful training that can foster the development of solid Christian characters in the lives of disciples. That which undermines the home, church, or school also undermines discipleship.

We live in an imperfect world where such undermining of faith happens on a regular basis. Homes break apart, churches suffer division, and schools encounter problems with students and personnel who fail to live up to Christian ideals. With so many challenges, how can we build strong homes, healthy churches, and vibrant schools? Mark 10 offers important instruction in this regard.

A healthy home

In the Judaism of Jesus' day, divorce was accepted for a variety of reasons—childlessness, material neglect, emotional neglect, and unfaithfulness.[1] Two passages in the Old Testament were used to justify divorce: Deuteronomy 24:1–4 and Exodus 21:10, 11. The first text describes a case-law situation, in which if a husband divorced his wife and she married another man, the first husband could not later remarry the woman if her second husband died or divorced her. The passage does not argue why divorce was permitted; it assumes that it was being practiced and limits the harm that could come to the woman.[2]

The text in Exodus 21:10, 11 at first blush does not seem to deal with the issue of divorce. However, it describes a case, in which if a man marries a slave girl and then marries another woman, he cannot reduce the allowances for clothing, food, or marital relations for the first wife. Otherwise, she goes out free from his house, implying the end of the marriage as well. This text does not command divorce but rather assumes that it happens in the imperfect setting of human relationships, again providing protection for the woman.

How did these passages become the basis for a general principle of divorce being acceptable? The rabbis had a method of reasoning known as *qol vakhomer* (literally, "light and heavy"). The principle argues from a minor case to a major case or vice versa. The argument went as follows: If this right is true for a slave woman as found in Exodus 21, then it is clearly true for a free woman as well. And if a free woman has these rights, then surely her husband does as well.[3]

When the Pharisees questioned Jesus in Mark 10:2–9, they did not challenge the various grounds for divorce but whether divorce itself was acceptable. It may seem odd since all or almost all Jews believed that divorce was acceptable on a variety of grounds. But when one recognizes that the Pharisees brought this question to Jesus while He was standing in Perea—a territory controlled by Herod Antipas—the exchange begins to make sense. John the Baptist had been beheaded for rebuking the king for marrying his brother's wife, Herodias. She had divorced her first husband and married Herod Antipas. If Jesus were to say that divorce is invalid, He could be reported to Herod with consequences similar to those suffered by John the Baptist. It was a sly plan that the Pharisees had concocted.

Jesus wends His way through the trap with a resulting rejection of divorce and an affirmation of marriage without giving an opportunity for the Pharisees to report Him to the king. It is not an easy feat. When the Pharisees accost Him with the question, "Is it lawful for a man to divorce his wife?" (verse 2), Jesus responds with a question of His own: "What did Moses command you?" (verse 3).

Tellingly, the Pharisees respond that "Moses *allowed* a man to write a certificate of divorce and to send her away" (verse 4; emphasis added). Deuteronomy 24 and Exodus 21 were not commands to divorce. There is no *command* anywhere in Scripture to divorce. As noted above, the cases in Deuteronomy and Exodus assumed the existence of divorce and limited the harm, particularly to the woman.

Jesus sweeps away the underlying assumptions and argumentation of the religious leaders, referring back to Genesis 1 and 2 to determine God's original plan for marriage. Jesus draws from both chapters to make His point. First, He notes that Moses gave the Israelites permission in Deuteronomy 24, not because it was God's will but because of their hard hearts. Hardly a good reason for breaking up a home. He then refers to Genesis 1:27, noting that God made humans in two forms—male and female. Moreover, His plan for these two human forms is that "a man shall leave his father and his mother and hold fast to his wife, and they shall become one flesh" (Genesis 2:24). Here Jesus asserts that the two individuals become one flesh in marriage, and what God has joined together, no person (the Greek word is *anthropos*, "a human being") should separate (see Mark 10:7–9).

This argumentation by Jesus has profound implications. First, He affirms the historical nature of the Creation account as found in Genesis 1 and 2. If those chapters do not report historical events, then Jesus' argument fails. Second, Jesus affirms that God's plan for marriage is between one man and one woman. Other arrangements do not fit within the biblical plan for life, disallowing same-sex marriage and polygamy. It is one man and one woman. Third, Jesus clearly views marriage as a lifelong commitment between husband and wife. It is this lifelong commitment that gives stability to the foundational building block of society—the home.

Elsewhere (Matthew 5:32; 19:9), Jesus makes allowance for divorce on the grounds of marital infidelity, but even there, He does not *require* a divorce. The all-too-common focus on exceptions—when is it permissible—undermines Jesus' emphasis on the stable home. We should not seek a change of spouse when we disagree but rather a change of heart. Humility, confession of sin, openness, kindness, and gentleness, in an atmosphere of committed fidelity, will give husband, wife, and children the kind of stability they need to grow into happy Christians and citizens.

Jesus and children

Children are valued in all societies; while the Greco-Roman society of Jesus' day valued and trained children, they also were not above leaving unwanted children to die in remote places or even throwing them on dunghills.[4] Judaism and early Christianity rejected such practices.[5]

Children liked Jesus, and He loved them. We have numerous examples in the Gospels of Jesus interacting with children. He raises the daughter of Jairus (Matthew 9:25; Mark 5:41–43; Luke 8:54–56), heals the daughter of the Syrophoenician woman (Matthew 15:21–28; Mark 7:24–30), casts a demon out of a boy (Matthew 17:14–21; Mark 9:14–29; Luke 9:37–43), and heals the son of a royal official (John 4:46–54). He calls a child to Him and uses him as an example of true discipleship while indicating that misleading such a young one would be a terrible crime (Matthew 18:1–6; Mark 9:35–37; Luke 9:47, 48). He accepts five loaves and two fish from a boy and feeds five thousand (John 6:9). Clearly, Jesus considers children important.

The disciples, for some reason, think that children should not take up Jesus' time. Becoming indignant, Jesus insists that they be allowed to come to Him. He places His hands on them and blesses them (Mark 10:13–16; Matthew 19:13–15; Luke 18:15–17). This brief passage shows that Christians are to place emphasis on the training and discipling of children. As a pastor, I have found the faith of young children preparing for baptism refreshing. The hands shoot up during our studies when I ask a commitment question, such as, "How many of you want Jesus to be your Savior?" "How many of you want to live your life for Jesus?" Enthusiastic hands again. No wonder Jesus used the simple faith of a child as the paradigm for Christian life.

The rich man and following Jesus

Jesus had a good deal to say about material things and riches. His call to the first disciples in Mark 1 illustrates the dedication required for His mission: "They left their nets and followed him" (verse 18). And in Mark 2:14, a similar experience occurs for Levi: "And he rose and followed him."

Teaching Disciples, Part 2

In Mark 10:17–22, a rich man (he is not called young in Mark nor a ruler) asks Him, "Good Teacher, what must I do to inherit eternal life?" (verse 17). It is the central question of life. Jesus first questions the man's reference to Him as "Good Teacher." Does the man know who Jesus is—the divine Son of God? Then Jesus refers to the last half of the Decalogue, implying that these commandments are the duty of one who wants to enter eternal life. The man claims to have kept all these commands from his youth. Only Mark tells us that Jesus looked at the man and loved him. There was something appealing about his idealism.

The man asked what he must do to inherit eternal life. Inheritance in the Old Testament was particularly focused on the land (Genesis 15:1–7). This eventually came to be seen to include inheriting the earth made righteous and renewed (Psalm 37; Isaiah 61; Matthew 5:5; 25:34; Revelation 21:7).[6] Inheritance involved both actions and a relationship. The question is whether the man recognizes the dual role—both relationship and action. He seems to focus on action.

Jesus puts him to the test and tells him to sell all that he has and follow Him. The sad report is that the man goes away disheartened, for he has great possessions. You see, money is seductive. It easily wraps a person up in making more and more for security, power, and prestige. It can entice almost anyone.

The way Jesus answers the man has troubled some since it seems to suggest that we are saved by good actions—by commandment keeping. Aren't we saved by grace through faith, apart from works (Ephesians 2:8–10)? Indeed, we are, but the Bible is just as clear that we are judged by our deeds (Proverbs 24:12; Isaiah 59:18; Jeremiah 50:29; Lamentations 3:64; Hosea 4:9; Matthew 16:27; 2 Corinthians 5:10; 2 Timothy 4:14; Revelation 22:12).

How do these two concepts fit together? The answer is

biblical anthropology. The Bible's anthropology is holistic. You do not have a soul; you are a soul—the combination of the "dust from the ground" and "the breath of life" (Genesis 2:7). As such, your inner faith reveals itself in your outward deeds. You do what you are. A lack of a faith relationship with God also reveals itself in outward actions. Thus, obedience is required of the Christian, but it is the *fruit* of a saving relationship, not the *root* of that relationship. The root is God's grace in your life. You cannot save yourself, as Jesus explains to His disciples in Mark 10:27: "With man it is impossible, but not with God. For all things are possible with God." The outgrowth of a saving relationship with God shows itself in acts of grace and mercy toward others (James 2:14–26).

"What do you want me to do for you?"

Mark 10 concludes with two interesting stories: two brothers who ask for the best seats, and a blind man who asks to receive his sight. The brothers, James and John, come to Jesus and ask Him to grant whatever they request. Jesus rightly asks them, "What do you want me to do for you?" (verse 36). What they want is to sit at His right and at His left in His kingdom. The Lord responds with another question: "Are you able to drink the cup that I drink, or to be baptized with the baptism with which I am baptized?" (verse 38). The cup will be Jesus' suffering in Gethsemane (Mark 14:36), and the baptism will be His death on the cross.[7]

The two brothers do not catch His meaning because they are angling for seats of honor. Jesus solemnly notes that they will drink His cup and be baptized with His baptism. James will be the first disciple to die by the sword, and John, the longest lived, will be exiled to Patmos.

The other disciples are rightly upset by the brothers' request. Jesus settles things down by clarifying the divine view of power. Power is not for the service of self but for service to others. Jesus caps it off by saying, "For even the Son of Man came not to be served but to serve, and to give his life as a ransom for many" (Mark 10:45).

The last story in the chapter is about a blind beggar named Bartimaeus who calls out for mercy. Jesus responds with the same question He put to the brothers who wanted special places in His kingdom: "What do you want me to do for you?" (verse 51). Rather than asking for a special privilege, Bartimaeus simply and earnestly asks to recover his sight. Jesus grants his request, and the blind man follows Him on the road.

The healing of Bartimaeus is a fitting bookend to this section on discipleship (Mark 8–10). Following Jesus is what we have been called to do. All around us are suffering people in need of our service. Jesus calls us to be His hands and His feet, faithfully ministering to His children.

---

1. See David Instone-Brewer, *Divorce and Remarriage in the Bible: The Social and Literary Context* (Grand Rapids, MI: Eerdmans, 2002), 85–132.

2. There are differences of opinion about why the husband could not remarry the woman. The most likely explanation is to prevent the husband from profiting twice from her dowry. See Richard D. Nelson, *Deuteronomy: A Commentary*, Old Testament Library (Louisville, KY: Westminster John Knox, 2002), 288, 289. See also Instone-Brewer, *Divorce and Remarriage*, 7; Raymond Westbrook, "Prohibition of Restoration of Marriage in Deuteronomy 24.1–4," in *Studies in Bible, 1986*, ed. S. Japhet, Scripta Hierosolymitana 31 (Jerusalem: Magnes, 1986), 387–405.

3. Instone-Brewer, *Divorce and Remarriage*, 101. This rabbinic argumentation is clearly viewed from a patrilineal perspective in which a husband would be viewed as superior in rights to women.

4. S. M. Baugh, "Marriage and Family in Ancient Greek Society," in *Marriage and Family in the Biblical World*, ed. Ken M. Campbell (Downers Grove, IL: InterVarsity, 2003), 123, 124. The exposure of infants led

to them being "rescued" sometimes, only to become part of the trade of raising unwanted infants to become slaves.

5. See Flavius Josephus, *Against Apion* 2.26; Philo, *On the Special Laws* 3.20.110–119. See also the discussion in Adela Yarbro Collins, *Mark*, Hermeneia (Minneapolis, MN: Fortress, 2007), 445, 446. For Christian texts, see Didache 2.2; 5.2; Barnabas 19.5; 20.1–2; Diognetus 5.6.

6. Extrabiblical texts of second-temple Judaism contain similar ideas. Psalms of Solomon 14:9, 10 presents the devout inheriting life in happiness while sinners inherit Hades and destruction. The Sibylline Oracles, lines 46–49, speak of those who honor God as living in the luxuriant garden of Paradise through all eternity. See Collins, *Mark*, 476.

7. There is a strong linkage between the scene of Jesus' baptism in Mark 1 and His death on the cross in Mark 15. Both locations have a figure like Elijah (John the Baptist in Mark 1, and a reference to Jesus calling Elijah in Mark 15), a declaration of who Jesus is, the Spirit coming and departing, and something torn (the heavens and the veil of the temple).

9

Jerusalem Controversies

We have now come to Jesus' crucial ministry in Jerusalem, including the final scenes of His earthly life (known as the Passion)—the Last Supper, Gethsemane, Jewish and Roman trials, His death on the cross, His burial, and the Resurrection. These chapters, Mark 11–16, cover about one week of time, whereas the previous ten chapters cover a period of approximately three and a half years. This slowing of the narrative indicates that the evangelist considers these closing scenes as the most crucial ones in the story.

This is rightly so since the focus of these chapters is Jesus' challenge to Jerusalem's leaders to turn to God and the leaders' response in calling for His crucifixion. For some people, these scenes are the tragic end of a good man's life. But that perspective misses the dual plot that runs throughout these chapters—the will of man versus the will of God. The will of man appears in the process of killing the Son of God. Yet the will of God triumphs when Jesus is crucified, buried, and resurrected.

When Jesus dies on the cross, He accepts the baptism of blood and becomes the "ransom for many" (Mark 10:38, 45), offering to us the cup of blessing (Mark 14:23–25) in place of the cup of suffering (verse 36). The will of God reaches its climax at the cross, and He affirms Christ's sacrifice in the Resurrection.

The triumphal entry

Just a few days before Calvary, Jesus' Jerusalem ministry begins with His triumphal entry, described in Mark 11. Jerusalem is located in the hill country of southern Palestine at an elevation of about twenty-four hundred feet, well above the Jordan Valley where Jericho sits near the Dead Sea. Jerusalem sits on several hills. In Jesus' day, the population may have been around forty or fifty thousand, small by modern standards. But in the Roman Empire of the era, it would have been a second-tier city, only below such cities as Rome, Alexandria, and Ephesus.

Jesus approaches the city from the east, coming over the Mount of Olives, which stands above the temple mount. Herod's temple dominated the city skyline.[1] The entire city covered about 250 acres, and the temple mount was 37 acres.[2] The temple accounted for about 15 percent of the total city area, but its massive and impressive structures overshadowed the rest of the city.

On the south side of the temple mount was the Royal Stoa—a covered colonnade supported by three rows of 162 large pillars. The circumference of each massive pillar was the measure of three men with outstretched arms and hands clasped. To the north, east, and west of the temple, there were covered colonnades as well, each with two rows of pillars. The one to the east was known as Solomon's Portico. On the north was the Antonio Fortress, where Roman troops were quartered, ready to quell any riot on the temple mount (cf. Acts 21). The temple mount was truly impressive.

The temple itself, at its largest points, was one hundred

cubits wide by one hundred cubits tall (a cubit was about 18 inches). The Holy Place of the temple was twenty cubits by forty cubits, and the Most Holy Place was twenty cubits by twenty cubits. The doorway into the temple was covered by a massive veil, which was embroidered with a depiction of the starry heavens. Another huge veil covered the entrance to the Most Holy Place. The temple was made from local limestone and decorated with gold.

Jesus enters the temple mount on His triumphal entry through one of the two gates on the east of the city, either through what is known as the Lion's Gate or, more likely, through the Golden Gate, which led directly onto the temple mount. It would have been easy for Jesus to incite a riot or wrest control of the temple, but He chooses not to do so. Instead, because it is late in the day, He retires with His disciples to Bethany (Mark 11:11).

The next morning Jesus and His disciples set forth to go to Jerusalem, only a few miles distant. Jesus is hungry and, seeing a fig tree in leaf, goes to find some early figs. This was not counted as stealing. People could satisfy their hunger from a neighbor's field or orchard, so Jesus' action is not unusual (Leviticus 19:9, 10; 23:22; Deuteronomy 23:25). However, He finds no fruit, for as Mark says, "it was not the season for figs" (Mark 11:13). But then, surprisingly, Jesus curses the tree in the hearing of His disciples. What could this mean?

In order to highlight the meaning, the story line pivots to Jesus entering the temple. (The word for temple used here is *hieron*, which refers to the entire temple mount complex, not the temple itself. For that building, the word is *naos*.) Jesus clears out those buying and selling on the temple grounds. This likely took place in the area of the Royal Stoa to the south of the temple itself. The Royal Stoa was a place where both Jews and Gentiles could go. Closer to the temple building was a low wall with inscriptions warning Gentiles not to proceed further on threat of death.

This action by Jesus—clearing the temple—creates animosity with the religious leaders. They begin to send groups to confront Him. This is where we have the controversy stories of Mark 11 and 12. But before briefly discussing these stories, it is important to make sense of the cursing of the fig tree and the cleansing of the temple.

The cursing of the fig tree, in combination with the cleansing of the temple, is the fourth of Mark's intercalations or sandwich stories.[3] The story stands in contrast to the cleansing of the temple. The irony is that the religious leaders resist the cleansing of the temple, plotting to do away with Jesus. And it is this plot that turns the cleansing of the temple into a curse. Jesus' death will bring the end of the significance of the temple sacrifices and portend the eventual destruction of the temple itself. This explains why the story of the cursed fig tree is folded into the story of the cleansing of the temple.

Conflict stories

After the cleansing of the temple, Jesus returns the next day (Tuesday of Passion Week), only to have the religious leaders confront Him concerning His actions the day before. They ask Him, "By what authority are you doing these things, or who gave you this authority to do them?" (Mark 11:28). They are not seeking an answer to their question; they want to trap Him with His answer. But Jesus outwits them, asking them a question about John the Baptist's baptism: Was it from heaven or man?

Too late they realize that their trap has been turned on them because whatever answer they give will put them in trouble. If they affirm that his baptism was from heaven, then they will need to accept his message. If they deny his baptism, they will jeopardize their standing with the people, who view

John as a prophet. In the face of this dilemma, they opt to lie and say they do not know where John's baptism came from. This allows Jesus to leave their question unanswered.

But He is not done. He tells the strange parable of the tenant farmers (Mark 12:1–11). The Lord begins the parable with a description of a vineyard being established by a man. The description has strong parallels to the parable of the vineyard in Isaiah 5. Anyone acquainted with the Old Testament prophet would recognize the linkage. This linkage would say to the listeners that the vineyard represented Israel (Isaiah 5:7). Clearly, the tenant farmers represented the Jewish religious leaders; the planter of the vineyard represented God; and the beloved son represented Jesus, the Son of God.

Mark 12:12 indicates that the religious leaders recognize that Jesus has told the parable "against them"—the illogical and greedy tenants. Their plot to kill Jesus will, according to the parable, result in their destruction. It is actually a merciful warning from Jesus, showing the leaders where their steps are leading. But they fail to heed the warning, choosing to continue their plot to destroy Him.

Taxes

Two other controversies appear in Mark 12: the question of paying taxes to Caesar and the question of the resurrection. The Pharisees come to Jesus with a question about taxes: "Is it lawful to pay taxes to Caesar, or not? Should we pay them, or should we not?" (verse 14). As before, it is not that they are seeking information from Jesus. Rather, they are hoping to trap Him in His words. In their estimation, there is no good answer to the question. If Jesus says to pay the taxes, they will discredit Him with the common people who hate the Romans and their taxes. If He says not to pay, they will get Him in trouble with the Romans.

Jesus' response is brilliant: "Render to Caesar the things

that are Caesar's, and to God the things that are God's" (verse 17). Many Christians have wondered over the years just how to relate to earthly governments, particularly ones that break away from the fear of the Lord. The biblical perspective is that God sets up governments and takes them down (Daniel 5:17–21; Romans 13:1–7). God grants power to human beings to bless and protect others, keep order, and punish evil (1 Peter 2:13–17). "Render [*apodidōmi*, "give back, pay"] to Caesar the things that are Caesar's" is Jesus' statement of this principle. We are to respect the authorities under which we live and pay our just taxes.

The second part of the statement—render "to God the things that are God's"—indicates another duty, a higher one, requiring our supreme allegiance. Just a few verses later, Jesus quotes from Deuteronomy 6:5: "You shall love the Lord your God with all your heart and with all your soul and with all your mind and with all your strength" (Mark 12:30).

Drawing on this principle, the apostles, when charged by the religious leaders to stop preaching about Jesus, responded by saying: "We must obey God rather than men" (Acts 5:29). Ellen White summarizes this nicely: Jesus "declared that since they were living under the protection of the Roman power, they should render to that power the support it claimed, so long as this did not conflict with a higher duty. But while peaceably subject to the laws of the land, they should at all times give their first allegiance to God."[4]

The resurrection

The other controversy story in Mark 12 is about the resurrection—a dispute brought by the Sadducees. They were a priestly aristocratic group.[5] They were in control of the temple services and were the opponents of the Pharisees. They believed only in the five books of Moses and did not believe in resurrection from the dead.

They come to Jesus with a conundrum story, probably a hypothetical situation, designed to mock belief in the resurrection.

> And they asked him a question, saying, "Teacher, Moses wrote for us that if a man's brother dies and leaves a wife, but leaves no child, the man must take the widow and raise up offspring for his brother. There were seven brothers; the first took a wife, and when he died left no offspring. And the second took her, and died, leaving no offspring. And the third likewise. And the seven left no offspring. Last of all the woman also died. In the resurrection, when they rise again, whose wife will she be? For the seven had her as wife" (verses 18–23).

So the Sadducees posit that all seven brothers end up marrying the same woman (based on Deuteronomy 25:5–10) without leaving any heir, and last of all, the woman dies after a long life. Their question is this: Whose wife will she be in the resurrection since all the brothers had her as a wife? They are attempting to discredit the resurrection, showing that it promotes immorality (seven men with one woman).

Jesus sweeps away their hypocrisy with a twofold argument. First, He states that when the dead rise, they neither marry nor are given in marriage. Notice the three aspects of Christ's answer.

1. He flatly states that the dead rise back to life.
2. He notes that they do not marry. In this patrilineal society, Jesus is addressing the action of the man in seeking and marrying a wife.
3. He dismisses the idea of new marriages in heaven. To be "given in marriage" was the action taken by the bride's father in agreeing to the marriage, and that will not happen in heaven.

But what about existing marriages? Jesus does not address this, though in the context of the argument, it seems clear that He is stating that there will be no marriages in heaven. This statement has raised many questions about our happiness in heaven—questions that can only be answered after Jesus returns. But one thing is certain, our relationships in heaven will meet and exceed our expectations. We can trust Him to care for us because He knows what will make us happy.

The second part of Jesus' response to the Sadducees draws scriptural support for the resurrection from the Pentateuch, Moses' five books. He quotes from Exodus 3:6—a passage that the Sadducees accepted as authoritative—noting God's declaration that He is "the God of Abraham, and the God of Isaac, and the God of Jacob" (Mark 12:26). Jesus is simply saying that because of the resurrection, these patriarchs will live again. God is not the God of the dead but of the living.

In this line of thinking, Jesus is consistent with the rabbinic principle of argumentation: what the general term affirms is also true of the particular. This is so because the particular is an example of the general. In this case, since God is the God of the living (the general term), it must also be true that He is the God of Abraham, Isaac, and Jacob (the particular term). Thus, these patriarchs, along with the rest of the righteous dead, will rise again in the resurrection.

---

1. See Ehud Netzer, *The Architecture of Herod, the Great Builder* (Grand Rapids, MI: Baker, 2008), 137–178. Also see Flavius Josephus, *Antiquities of the Jews* 15.11.3–7; Flavius Josephus, *Jewish War* 5.5.1–6; m. Middot. The details of the accounts in Josephus and the Mishnah are open to differing interpretations.

2. William Horbury, W. D. Davies, and John Sturdy, eds., *The Cambridge History of Judaism*, vol. 3, *The Early Roman Period* (Cambridge, UK: Cambridge University Press, 1999), 43.

3. See chapter 3 of this book for a more detailed description of this storytelling technique.

4. Ellen G. White, *The Desire of Ages* (Mountain View, CA: Pacific Press®, 1940), 602.

5. See Everett Ferguson, *Backgrounds of Early Christianity*, 3rd ed. (Grand Rapids, MI: Eerdmans, 2003), 519, 520.

10

The Last Days

After Jesus finished His arguments with the religious leaders, described in Mark 11 and 12, He sat down in the treasury area of the temple and watched people bring their offerings (Mark 12:41–44). The temple complex had thirteen chests with horn-shaped openings that received the different offerings. Exactly where these chests were located is disputed.[1] Perhaps they were located in various parts of the temple complex. In any case, Mark 12:41 indicates that Jesus was sitting opposite the treasury, located in the Court of the Women, near the temple building itself.

As He watched the people putting in their offerings, he noticed that some of them deposited large sums. Soon a widow approached and threw in two *lepta*. The *lepton*, the singular of *lepta*, was the smallest coin in use in Palestine in Jesus' day. It took 64 lepta to equal one denarius. The denarius was the day's wage of a day laborer, like the ones Jesus described in the parable of the vineyard (Matthew 20:1–16).

To arrive at a current value for the widow's offering, simply divide a day's wages by 64. It does not amount to much! Furthermore, Jesus noted that these two lepta were all the widow had and all she had to live on.

It is striking—the contrast between the rich gifts given by the many versus the very small amount given by the one widow. In today's setting, we would not likely notice what the widow had given, but Jesus did. The truth of the matter is that we see what a person puts in the offering plate, but God sees what is left in that person's pocket. In proportional terms, the widow gave the most because she gave everything.

Great lessons flow from this short story. First, Jesus affirmed supporting the work of God with our offerings. Yes, the temple leaders were corrupt, as we have seen in Jesus' cleansing of the temple and His dispute with the religious leaders. But that corruption did not tarnish the gift of the widow. God blesses her, even though the religious leaders were not upright.

Some people hold back their tithes and offerings when they think the money is being used incorrectly. This is a mistake. Individuals who do so miss the blessing. Religious leaders have a responsibility to use donations wisely and ethically, but even if they fail to do so, God blesses those who give faithfully. Otherwise, our gifts would have strings attached and would not be free of our control.

Second, everyone has a part to play in supporting the work of God, rich and poor alike. Some people think the poor should not be called upon to give offerings and that they should be the recipients of the gifts. While giving to the poor is blessed by God, the poor themselves also have a role to play in supporting God's work. Otherwise, we subtly depreciate them and suggest that they are not wise enough or rich enough to support the work of God and that such support is better left to their wiser and richer brothers and sisters. But Scripture does not support such an idea. Tithes and offerings are for everyone to give. We are all equal before God, and all are called to support God's cause.

Third, giving to the cause of God sets us free from the slavery of covetousness. Money is seductive (remember the rich ruler who did not follow Jesus in Mark 10:17–22) and can easily wed itself to the heart, deadening our sensitivity to the needs of others. Giving regularly helps to root out the selfishness that diminishes our lives. Giving back to God indicates that possessions do not rule us and that we let them go for Him to reuse. Our characters are shaped by this habit of giving, thus enriching our lives.

The end is not yet

After Jesus watched people giving money in the temple, He departed, likely exiting through the Golden Gate on the east side of the temple complex, heading toward the Mount of Olives. One of His disciples pointed out the great and amazing buildings of the temple mount (Mark 13:1). Jesus responded, "Do you see these great buildings? There will not be left here one stone upon another that will not be thrown down" (verse 2).

Such a statement by Jesus had to completely shock the disciples. The temple mount had structures and stones that were massive, built at great expense and labor. It had taken nearly fifty years to bring the temple complex to the beauty it enjoyed in the AD 30s. To imagine its destruction would be like someone suggesting that the largest structure in one's country would be demolished. It just seemed unbelievable.

As Jesus sat opposite the temple on the Mount of Olives (verses 3, 4), Peter, James, John, and Andrew asked Him for more details. It is important to remember their question: "Tell us, when will these things be, and what will be the sign when all these things are about to be accomplished?" (verse 4). Jesus answered their questions in the rest of Mark 13, which is the longest connected speech by Jesus in the entire book of Mark. Jesus' discourse can be divided into four parts:

The Last Days

1. The signs of the end of the age, in response to the disciples' questions (verses 1–13)
2. The destruction of Jerusalem and the Tribulation (verses 14–23)
3. The coming of the Son of Man (verses 24–27)
4. The eschatological lessons to be learned (verses 28–37)

Space does not allow us to delve into the details of this passage, but we will discuss key topics in Jesus' discourse that help us understand His teaching. In the first section (verses 1–13), Jesus' key prediction is found in verse 2: "There will not be left here one stone upon another that will not be thrown down." In verse 4, the disciples ask a question that has two parts: a temporal aspect regarding the *when* of the events and an action aspect concerning *what* events would portend the destruction of the temple.

What stands out in this first section is Jesus' major emphasis on warning, even as He gives predictions. He does not begin in verse 5 with either the *when* or the *what*. Instead, He focuses on what could mislead them from recognizing the signs of the times. They must not let anyone lead them astray (verse 5), they must not be alarmed by news of wars (verse 7), they must be on their guard because they will be persecuted (verse 9), and they must not be anxious about being brought before leaders (verse 11).

Of course, Jesus does make certain predictions about events leading up to the destruction of Jerusalem. These include false messiahs (verse 6), wars and rumors of wars (verse 7), earthquakes and famines (verse 8), persecution of the disciples (verse 9), the preaching of the gospel everywhere (verse 10), family members betraying believers (verse 12), and salvation for those who endure (verse 13).

In our day, many take Jesus' statements here to be a reference to the end of the world. However, the primary focus is on events leading up to the destruction of Jerusalem, as described in verses 14–18. Having said that, it is also possible to see Jesus' predictions here in the light of typology, where an event at a local level has a wider and broader application in a more universal setting. Thus, the destruction of Jerusalem portends the end of the world.

The abomination of desolation

The fulcrum, or turning point, of the chapter comes in Mark 13:14: "But when you see the abomination of desolation standing where he ought not to be (let the reader understand), then let those who are in Judea flee to the mountains." And what is this "abomination of desolation"?[2] Numerous explanations have been given, but it is important to remember that the phraseology comes from various references in the book of Daniel (Daniel 8:13; 9:27; 11:31; 12:11).

In the prophecies of Daniel, many scholars see this phraseology linked to the history of Antiochus IV Epiphanes, the Seleucid ruler, who in 167 BC set up a pagan altar in the temple in Jerusalem and offered a pig on it. These scholars take what is called a *preterist* view of prophecy: the prophecy refers to the time of the writer, who is often writing after the fact and pretending to be a prophet from an earlier time period.

The problem with the preterist view of the prophecies of Daniel, particularly regarding the abomination of desolation, is twofold. First, none of the time figures in Daniel fit the history of Antiochus—not the 2,300 days, 1,260 days, 70 weeks, or other time periods. One would expect that if Daniel were written by someone referring to the history of Antiochus, they would get the dates right. The other problem is that Jesus indicates that the abomination of desolation is still future to His day, and He makes no statement that He is reapplying the prophecy.

What, then, does the abomination of desolation refer to? It likely refers to the standards, or banners, that the Roman soldiers carried when they came to put down the Jewish Revolt. These banners had pagan symbols, and the soldiers worshiped around them. This idolatry would be an abomination in Israel. This viewpoint is corroborated by Luke's description in Luke 21:20: "But when you see Jerusalem surrounded by armies, then know that its desolation is near" (NKJV).

It would seem to be too late to escape when the city was surrounded. But amazingly, when the Roman general Cestius came up against the city in AD 66, the Jews rallied and fought off the Romans. The Romans inexplicably withdrew, and the Jews returned triumphant to the city. We can assume that any Christian left in the city at that time would recognize the signal and escape.[3]

In the typology we have noted above, a historical event finds a later historical fulfillment in a broader or wider application. When it comes to the abomination of desolation, the later historical fulfillment refers to the rise of the antichrist power predicted in Daniel 7 and 8 and Revelation 13.

The great tribulation and the final signs

In Mark 13:19, Jesus makes this prediction: "For in those days there will be such tribulation as has not been from the beginning of the creation that God created until now, and never will be." What does this great tribulation refer to? We notice two details in verse 19 that help in the interpretation of the verse. Jesus shifts to the future tense, pointing to something more distant than what He has been talking about before this. Furthermore, in contrast to the use of the pronouns "this" and "these," which predominate in verses 1–13 (verses 2, 4, 8, 11, 13, 29, 30), when describing events closer to His time, the Lord uses "that" and "those" more regularly in the last half of the prophecy (verses 11, 17, 19, 24, 32), pointing to events more distant from His time.

Jesus speaks of the Tribulation being worse than anything else in history. It can hardly refer just to the disastrous fall of Jerusalem since there have been worse disasters before and after. We suggest instead that Jesus is referring to the longer period of persecution by the antichrist power, which occurred during the 1,260-day prophecy of Daniel 7:23–27 (cf. Daniel 8:9–14, Revelation 12; 13; 2 Thessalonians 2). This period of persecution stretched from AD 538 to 1798 and was shortened by the Protestant Reformation, just as Jesus predicted in Mark 13:20.

After these events, Jesus predicts more false messiahs, with a repeated warning to be on guard (verses 21–23). Then the Lord indicates that signs would appear in the heavens after the great tribulation, portending His return: "The sun will be darkened, and the moon will not give its light, and the stars will be falling from heaven" (verses 24, 25). Adventists believe that these signs were fulfilled in the Dark Day of May 19, 1780, and the great Leonid meteor shower of November 13, 1833. It is not that these events were supernatural but that the Lord predicted their occurrence. During the eighteenth and nineteenth centuries, interest in the Second Coming renewed, and the Advent movement began. The next event is the shaking of the powers in the heavens and the return of our Lord and Savior (verses 25, 26).

This generation and that day

Mark 13:30 has troubled many people because of the words "this generation will not pass away until all these things take place." Was Jesus mistaken? The answer is no. His prophecy came true.

The explanation of this conundrum is found in a comparison of verse 30 with verse 32. Verse 30 uses the phrase "this generation," whereas verse 32 refers to "that day." Just as we noted above, the words "this" and "these" predominate in verses 1–13 and "that" and "those" in the later verses of the chapter. What this means is that Jesus' prediction about "this generation" refers to the people living during the first century, up to the fall of Jerusalem in AD 70, whereas "that day" in verse 32 refers to a more distant event—His second coming.

One more note: Jesus' prophecy in Mark 13 begins with His own day and extends through the centuries to His return in glory. In other words, the prophecy goes from the time of the prophet (Jesus, in this case) to the time of the end (His return). This is clearly a historicist interpretation of prophecy and counters the other approaches to prophetic interpretation (preterist, in the time of the prophet; futurist, close to the end; and idealist, always true, repeating over and over).

---

1. See Vincent Taylor, *The Gospel According to St. Mark*, 2nd ed. (London: Macmillan, 1966), 496; Adela Yarbro Collins, *Mark*, Hermeneia (Minneapolis, MN: Fortress, 2007), 588, 589. For the description of the chests in the Mishnah, see m. Sheqalim 6.5.

2. See Tom Shepherd, "Abomination of Desolation," in *The New Interpreter's Dictionary of the Bible*, vol. 1, *A–C*, ed. Katharine Doob Sakenfeld (Nashville, TN: Abingdon, 2006), 16, 17. The same phraseological challenge is seen in Mark 13:14 as in Daniel since "abomination" is a neuter noun, but the word "standing," referring back to it, is masculine (cf. the ESV translation: "When you see the abomination of desolation standing where *he* ought not to be" [emphasis added]).

3. The church historian Eusebius, writing in the fourth century, indicates that the Christians in Jerusalem were warned by an oracle to escape to Pella and that they did so before the war began. See Eusebius, *Church History* 3.5.3; Epiphanius, *Panarion* 29.7.7; Epiphanius, *On Weights and Measures* 15.

11

Taken and Tried

Chapters 14–16 of Mark are designated as the Passion narrative because they tell the story of Jesus' last supper with His disciples, His struggle in the Garden of Gethsemane, His Jewish and Roman trials, His crucifixion, His burial, and His resurrection. The word *Passion* is used because of its linkage with the Greek word *paschō*, which means "to suffer."

In this chapter, we will look at the events described in Mark 14. The evangelist uses a spare, straightforward style that seems to make readers present, watching the events take place. There is little commentary added, likely because Mark saw this as the most compelling way to show the power of Jesus' death and resurrection.

We noted in chapter 9 that the last six chapters of Mark (Mark 11–16) occur during only approximately one week of time, whereas the previous ten chapters occur over about three and a half years. The slowing of narrative time shows that the evangelist considers these final events of Jesus' life on Earth to be the center of attention. That attention is even more focused in these last three chapters—Mark 14–16.

Determining the exact chronology of the events described

in Mark 14–16 has certain challenges, particularly related to comparing the descriptions in Matthew, Mark, and Luke with the description in the Gospel of John.[1] All the Gospels agree that Jesus died on a Friday (called the Preparation Day in the Gospels), that He lay in the tomb over the Sabbath, and that He rose on Sunday morning. In Matthew, Mark, and Luke, Jesus' last supper with His disciples is clearly referred to as a Passover meal (Matthew 26:17–25; Mark 14:12–21; Luke 22:7–23). In the Jewish calendar, that meal would be eaten during the night portion of the fifteenth day of Nisan.[2] This was clearly the night before Jesus' crucifixion. So, in this reckoning, Jesus was crucified on the afternoon, or day portion, of Nisan 15.

However, in John 18:28, we are told that the religious leaders did not enter Pilate's headquarters so that they would not be defiled and thus prevented from eating the Passover. John does not describe Jesus' last supper as a Passover meal. It appears that the Synoptic Gospels indicate what Jesus *did*—He ate the Passover on Thursday night—and John tells us what the religious leaders *had not done* on Friday morning. The problem is that the Passover meal had to be eaten on the night of Nisan 15, and any leftovers of the meal were to be burned before the next morning (Exodus 34:25; Numbers 9:12).

There have been numerous explanations for the apparent discrepancy between the Synoptic Gospels and John. It could be that Jesus ate a preemptive Passover meal, different groups ate the Passover at different times, or Jesus was instituting a "new Passover" with the Lord's Supper.[3] Any of these solutions resolves the apparent discrepancy between the Synoptic Gospels and John. The issues involved here are complex, however, and the *Seventh-day Adventist Bible Commentary* has an excellent article on the chronology of Jesus' life.[4]

Unforgettable

Mark 14:1–11 presents the fifth sandwich story in the Gospel of Mark (see chapter 3 for more details explaining this storytelling technique). In the two stories at the beginning of Mark 14, two parallel people, both disciples of Jesus, do opposite actions—one betraying Him and the other honoring Him. Both events are unforgettable.

In Mark 14:1, 2, the religious leaders are looking for a way to put Jesus to death, but they do not want to arrest Him in public because that would cause a riot. They have a plan they want to carry out, but they are not sure of a method to arrest Jesus away from the crowd. Their need will be supplied by a most unusual and unforgettable source: one of the disciples of Jesus, indeed, one of the Twelve—Judas Iscariot.

The story of the priests and Judas pauses, and the inner story of the sandwich commences in verse 3. It, too, presents an unforgettable story, not because of a named person but rather because of what Jesus says. An unnamed woman anoints Jesus' head with very expensive nard ointment. No reason is given for her actions, and she never says a word in the narrative.

This drama takes place in Bethany, which is about two miles (3.2 kilometers) from Jerusalem. Jesus is at the home of Simon the leper. The Greek term for *leprosy* here is *lepros*, referring to a variety of skin diseases—psoriasis, seborrhea, eczema, lupus, and so on—not simply what we would call leprosy or Hansen's disease today.[5] A person with such a disease would be ceremonially unclean. The fact that Simon was able to host this dinner suggests that he had been cleansed of leprosy.[6] Ellen White implies that he had been healed by Jesus, and this was the reason he held a feast in honor of the Lord.[7]

The woman's gift was extravagant, worth nearly a year's wages for a day laborer. However, the container for the perfume was also costly, as it was made of alabaster.[8] The perfume was made from nard, which came from present-day India and Nepal, therefore, making it very costly.[9] Those at the feast find her gift a waste. They, thereby, express their valuation of Jesus, whereas the woman has expressed her valuation by her action. She broke the neck of the alabaster flask, thus committing the entire amount to her anointing of Jesus.

When someone does an amazing action like this, people who do not participate are shamed. Not uncommonly, to cover that shame, those people blame the person who gave the gift. This is exactly what happens here: shame is disguised by supposed care for the poor. But Jesus comes to the defense of the woman and notes two points: she has anointed Him for burial, and her action will be remembered forever as part of the gospel message (Mark 14:6–9). In fact, she is the only person in Mark that is said to have anointed Him for burial. The women who came on Sunday morning were too late because He had already risen.

The outer story is reentered in Mark 14:10 with Judas's nefarious action of betraying his Master to His enemies, all for the promise of money. The contrast between the two disciples—Judas and the unnamed woman—is displayed in the following chart:

Judas	Woman
Male	Female
Named; one of the Twelve	Unnamed disciple
Priests rejoice at his news	People censure the woman
Betrays Jesus to death	Anoints Jesus for burial
Promise of money	Gift worth > 300 denarii
Opportune time (*eukairōs*) to betray	Part of good news (*euaggelion*)

The irony between these two characters is best shown by

the play on the word *good*. The woman has done a "beautiful thing" (*kalos*) to Jesus, and her action is enshrined as part of the good news (*euaggelion*). Judas is doing the opposite of good but is looking for a "good" or opportune time (*eukairōs*) to betray Jesus. As noted before, the two plots are intertwined with one another. The plot of man (with the priests and Judas) is to bring Jesus to death. The plot of God (with the woman) is to bring the good news to the world.

The Lord's Supper and Gethsemane

In the Gospel of Mark, what we call the Last Supper was a Passover meal. Jesus instituted the Lord's Supper during this meal (Mark 14:22–25). He used bread and "the fruit of the vine" to create a new festival for His followers (verse 25).[10] The Lord symbolically called these His body and His blood. He refers to the cup as "my blood of the covenant, which is poured out for many" (verse 24).

The use of the phrase "blood of the covenant" alludes to the Sinai covenant that God made with Israel. Following the giving of the Ten Commandments and further commands (Exodus 20–23), Moses had young men offer sacrifices to God (Exodus 24:5). The Israelites then agreed to obey God (verse 7). Then Moses took blood from the sacrifices and threw it on the people, saying, "Behold the blood of the covenant that the LORD has made with you in accordance with all these words" (verse 8). The blood sealed the covenant between God and the Israelites.

Jesus significantly calls the cup "My blood of the covenant." He is the sacrifice that seals the new covenant with God. Jesus' words in Mark 14 remind us of His statement in Mark 10:45: "For even the Son of Man came not to be served but to serve, and to give his life as a ransom for many." This language is clearly substitutionary. Where we have failed in sin, He comes to our aid with His blood, covering our sins and bringing us into a new covenant relationship with God. It is truly a significant experience to take part in the Lord's Supper. We should always rejoice in its blessing and look forward to partaking in it.

After the Lord's Supper, Jesus went with His disciples (less Judas) to the Garden of Gethsemane. This garden was on the Mount of Olives, though the exact location is unknown since the Romans cut down all the trees when they besieged the city in AD 70.[11] Jesus warned His disciples that they would all fall away (Mark 14:27, 28). Peter insisted that he would not, but Jesus gave him a solemn warning that he would deny his Lord three times before the rooster crowed twice (verse 30). Peter again insisted that he would not deny Jesus.

In the Garden, Jesus became sorrowful and more and more isolated from His disciples. He prayed, and they slept. He came to them three times, seeking their support, but they slept through it all. It is in this garden that He accepted, from His Father's hand, the mysterious cup of suffering (verse 36).

In the Old Testament, the term *cup* has a metaphoric use and often refers to the cup of God's wrath (Psalm 75:8; Jeremiah 25:15–29; Ezekiel 23:31–34; Habakkuk 2:16).[12] That is probably what is in view here in Mark 14:36. Jesus took the cup from the Father's hand and decided to carry through with the sacrifice that would save humanity. As 1 Peter 2:23 states, Jesus "continued entrusting himself to him who judges justly." It was this decision that carried Jesus through all the injustices that He endured, up to and including the cross.

Jesus' and Peter's trial

Mark 14:53–72 is the final sandwich story in the Gospel of Mark. It is probably the most notable of all since the two parallel characters are Jesus and Peter. The trial of Jesus was an exercise in frustration for the religious leaders as they could not even get their false witnesses to agree. Finally, the high priest accosted Jesus with the direct question, "Are you the Christ, the Son of the Blessed?" (verse 61).

Jesus' answer was clarion and direct: "I am, and you will see the Son of Man seated at the right hand of Power, and coming with the clouds of heaven" (verse 62). It is this response that brought Him condemnation and a death sentence.

Some of those there began to spit on Him, covering His face and striking Him with the mocking cry, "Prophesy!" (verse 65).

In Mark 14:66, the narrative cuts back to the story of Peter, who was below in the courtyard. Confronted by a servant girl, he twice denied that he knew Jesus (verses 68, 70). Finally, challenged by bystanders, Peter called down a curse on himself if he was not telling the truth and emphatically said, "I do not know this man of whom you speak" (verse 71). But then the rooster crowed, and the words of Jesus' prediction came back to him—he would deny his Lord. Suddenly, he realized that he had done exactly what Jesus said he would do, and the revelation of his own perfidy cut him to the heart, and he broke down and wept.

As sad as Peter's story is—and this could easily happen to any of us—a deep irony in the story reveals who Jesus is. The leaders mockingly called on Him to prophesy (verse 65), even as one of His prophecies was coming true in the courtyard below. Peter's denial of Jesus, as it turns out, proved that Jesus was the Messiah. Again, the two plots of the Passion narrative drama are on display. Men thought they were convicting a charlatan, while in fact, the will of God for the salvation of the world was coming to fruition through the sacrifice of His Son.

---

1. Matthew, Mark, and Luke are called the Synoptic Gospels ("to see together") because their stories of Jesus' life, the order of the stories, and

the way the stories are told are so similar. Many scholars maintain that Matthew and Luke used Mark's Gospel as a source for their writing.

2. Seventh-day Adventists know that the Sabbath begins at sunset on Friday and extends to sunset on Saturday. In biblical reckoning, all days begin at sunset, even from the beginning. Genesis 1:5 states, "And there was *evening* and there was *morning*, the first day" (emphasis added).

3. Mark L. Strauss, *Mark*, Zondervan Exegetical Commentary on the New Testament (Grand Rapids, MI: Zondervan, 2014), 617, 618.

4. Francis D. Nichol, ed., *The Seventh-day Adventist Bible Commentary*, vol. 5 (Washington, DC: Review and Herald®, 1980), 235–266, esp. 248–265.

5. See Frederick W. Danker, Walter Bauer, William F. Arndt, and F. Wilbur Gingrich, *A Greek-English Lexicon of the New Testament and Other Early Christian Literature*, 3rd ed. (Chicago: University of Chicago Press, 2000), s.v. "*lepra, lepros.*" See also David P. Wright and Richard N. Jones, "Leprosy," in *The Anchor Bible Dictionary*, ed. David Noel Freedman (New Haven, CT: Yale University Press, 1992), 4:277–282.

6. See Strauss, *Mark*, 606.

7. Ellen G. White, *The Desire of Ages* (Mountain View, CA: Pacific Press®, 1940), 557.

8. See Strauss, *Mark*, 606, 607. Pliny the Elder states, "Unguents keep best in boxes of alabaster, and perfumes when mixed with oil, which conduces all the more to their durability the thicker it is, such as the oil of almonds, for instance." *The Natural History*, vol. 3, trans. John Bostock and H. T. Riley (London: Henry G. Bohn, 1855), 166 [13.3].

9. See Victor H. Matthews, "Perfumes and Spices," in *The Anchor Bible Dictionary*, ed. David Noel Freedman (New Haven, CT: Yale University Press, 1992), 5:226–228; R. T. France, *The Gospel of Mark*, New International Greek Testament Commentary (Grand Rapids, MI: Eerdmans, 2002), 551.

10. The word for "wine"—*oinos*—is never used in reference to the Lord's Supper throughout the New Testament. It is always either "the cup" or "the fruit of the vine," suggesting that this was not alcoholic wine but grape juice.

11. See Josephus, *Jewish Wars* 6.1.1; Raymond E. Brown, *The Death of the Messiah*, Anchor Bible Reference Library (New York: Doubleday, 1994), 1:149.

12. See Joel Marcus, *Mark 8–16*, Anchor Bible 27A (New Haven, CT: Yale University Press, 2009), 978.

12

Tried and Crucified

Mark 15 presents the Roman trial, the mockery of Jesus by the Roman soldiers, His crucifixion and humiliation, and His burial. This chapter is the center of the Passion narrative. The Evangelist presents it, as before, in stark detail with little comment since this method of presentation carries its own telling weight.

Jesus was brought before Pontius Pilate, who was the governor of Judea from AD 26 to 36. More accurately, he would be called a prefect. His tribal name was Pontius, and his family name was Pilate. But his personal name has not been preserved.[1]

Overall, the Roman Empire was divided administratively into two types of provinces: the senatorial provinces where the administrative head was known as a proconsul, who was appointed by the Roman Senate for a one-year term that could be renewed, and the imperial provinces that were under the direct rule of the emperor with a legate or prefect as the administrator.[2] Senatorial provinces were more peaceful, and the imperial provinces were more likely to have uprisings and require firmer control. Judea was one of the smaller imperial provinces.

Pilate was a ruthless man who ruled with a heavy hand. Luke 13:1 tells of him killing some Galileans when they were making sacrifices to God. And Josephus notes that Pilate took money from the temple treasury to help construct an aqueduct.[3] It was before this ruthless man that Jesus was brought for trial.

In the Jewish trial, the charge against Jesus was blasphemy, but that would not carry weight with the Romans. Mark 15 does not indicate what the charge was against Jesus, but the question that Pilate asked Him in Mark 15:2—"Are you the King of the Jews?"—gives a strong indication that Jesus was being charged with sedition against the Roman government for claiming to be a king. Apparently, this charge of sedition was what the religious leaders brought to Pilate, likely arising from Jesus' claim to be the Messiah ("anointed one"). Since kings in the Old Testament were anointed, it is not difficult to see how Jesus' claim to be the Messiah could be twisted.

Jesus was quiet and passive in His trial, to the amazement of the governor. Even in answering Pilate's question about being the king of the Jews, Jesus' response was noncommittal: "You have said so" (verse 2). In other words, "You are the one who has said that." It neither denied nor affirmed the title. Jesus did not respond to all the charges brought against Him. Though the Evangelist does not cite Isaiah 53, that chapter's reference to a sheep being silent before its shearers and the Servant of the Lord not opening His mouth seems a likely background.

Pilate was apparently unconvinced by the religious leaders' accusations, perhaps in light of Jesus' nonresponse. He sought a way out of the predicament by suggesting the release of a prisoner at the time of the Passover (Mark 15:6–9). Pilate recognized that the religious leaders had some plot against Jesus because of envy (verse 10). But what he did not recognize was that the leaders could easily stir up the crowd to destroy Jesus. This is exactly what they did, and the ambivalent Pilate gave in to their demand, sending an innocent man to His death.

Scourged and mocked

Having been convicted of sedition as a pretender to the throne, Jesus was sentenced to crucifixion. Mark indicates that Pilate scourged Jesus (verse 15). It was not likely Pilate himself who did this but rather his soldiers. In preparation for execution, the Romans used their most severe form of whipping, known as *verberatio*.[4] Roman soldiers would remove the convicted person's clothes and whip him with leather whips in which sharp objects, such as glass, stones, nails, or pieces of bone, were embedded. This would rip open the skin of the convicted person. Then they would reclothe the person.

The soldiers tasked with crucifying Jesus first led Him into the governor's headquarters and proceeded to mock Him by clothing Him in royal purple and placing a crown of thorns on His head. Thus, they combined signs of honor (the robe and crown) with signs of shame (the thorny crown and mockery). They called out the entire battalion for this purpose. A battalion (Greek *speira*) was one-tenth of a legion of six thousand men. But it could range from two hundred to six hundred men, which is still a large number.[5] Their mockery included hailing Jesus as "King of the Jews," striking His head with a reed, spitting on Him, and mockingly kneeling before Him.

Jesus bore all of this in silence. How was He able to do this? He had handed Himself over to the Father's will and trusted His Father's plan (1 Peter 2:21–25). The will of man was coming to fruition, but so was the will of God to save the world.

Crucified

Jesus' death on the cross has become the symbol of

Christian faith, and rightly so. Churches are decorated with the cross, and people wear it as jewelry and speak of it in everyday conversation (for example, "That was such a cross for me to bear"). But in the first century, it was not so. Crucifixion was so terrible that the Roman writer Seneca argued that suicide was preferable.[6]

The Romans usually crucified people naked to add to their shame.[7] Typically, they had the person carry the crossbeam, called the *patibulum*, to the site of crucifixion while naked. The upright portion of the cross, called the *stipes*, was usually left in the ground at the site. Mark 15:20 indicates that Jesus wore His clothes to the site of the crucifixion. The Jews hated public nakedness, so Jesus may have been allowed a loincloth for modesty. However, at Golgotha, the soldiers gambled for His clothing, so He may indeed have been crucified naked.

Jesus was unable to carry His cross, likely from exhaustion and from the beating He had received. In His stead, Simon of Cyrene was compelled to bear His cross. At Golgotha, they offered Jesus a stupefying drink, which He rejected.

Individuals were crucified either by being tied to the cross or nailed to it. We know that Jesus was nailed to the cross because of His encounter with Thomas, recorded in John 20. Thomas insisted that he would not believe in the Resurrection unless he put his hand in the mark of the nails, and Jesus invited him to do that very thing.

A crucifixion did not shed great amounts of blood. No major veins or arteries were severed in the process. The nails were not placed in the center of the hand since there were no structures there capable of bearing the weight of the body. Instead, the nails were driven through the base of the palm where the carpal bones could bear more weight. In the process of driving the nails, the median nerve that serves the hand would be crushed or severed. This could produce a clawlike grip. Any movement would send searing pain through the severed nerve to the arm. To get a good breath, the crucified person had to rotate his body around the nailed hands, which would create searing pain.[8]

Crucified persons often stayed alive for days, slowly dying from bleeding, exhaustion, and asphyxiation. They were exposed to the elements and would be food for wild dogs and birds.[9] It was truly a terrible way to die.

But for Jesus, it was an even heavier weight because He bore the sins of the world while enduring the mockery, the shame, and the pain. Ellen White describes His despair as He died on the cross: "With the terrible weight of guilt He bears, He cannot see the Father's reconciling face. The withdrawal of the divine countenance from the Saviour in this hour of supreme anguish pierced His heart with a sorrow that can never be fully understood by man. So great was this agony that His physical pain was hardly felt."[10]

Added to the suffering that Jesus experienced from the physical and spiritual aspects of His crucifixion was the mocking by those around the cross. The religious leaders, in particular, are singled out in Mark 15:31, 32. Their words are telling: "He saved others; he cannot save himself. Let the Christ, the King of Israel, come down now from the cross that we may see and believe." In mocking Jesus, the leaders contrasted His ministry with His current condition. Unknowingly, they were acknowledging Him as the Savior: "He saved others." The word for "save" here is *sōzō*—a verb that means "to heal, rescue, save." They were likely referring to Jesus' healing ministry, but the striking irony at the foot of the cross is that the enemies of Jesus declared Him to be the Savior. It is at the cross that the revelation aspect of the revelation-secrecy motif comes to a climax. The Christological titles now appear in public—Christ, King of the Jews, and King of Israel. The secrecy side of the motif will find its climax at the Resurrection in Mark 16.

Tried and Crucified

According to Mark 15:25, Jesus was crucified at the third hour of the day. This would have been about 9:00 A.M. From the sixth hour (noon) to the ninth hour (3:00 P.M.), the land was covered with darkness (verse 33). This darkness was not caused by an eclipse of the sun for two reasons. First, an eclipse of the sun is only possible during the new moon when the moon lines up with the sun. But Passover occurs at full moon, when the moon is in just the opposite location, on the far side of the earth from the sun. Second, during a total eclipse of the sun, it is quite dark, but that only occurs for a few minutes, not hours. This was a supernatural darkness.

Jesus cried out, "My God, my God, why have you forsaken me?" (verse 34). These are His only words from the cross in the Gospel of Mark. They are known as the cry of dereliction because of their great sorrow and despair. Actually, they are a prayer in which Jesus cried out to His Father with the words of Psalm 22:1. That psalm alternates back and forth between despair and praise of God. Both Matthew and Mark present the dark side of the cross—the deep cost to God to save the world. Luke and John present the light side of the cross—the great benefit that comes to us as a result of this salvation.

The scene of the cross in Mark 15 is parallel to Jesus' baptism in Mark 1. The parallelism consists of five elements:

Mark 1:9–11: The Baptism	Mark 15:34–39: The Cross
John baptizes Jesus	Jesus' baptism (cf. Mark 10:38)
John (Elijah figure, Mark 9:11–13)	Calling Elijah
Heavens split	Veil split
Spirit (Greek **Pneuma**)	Jesus expires (Greek *ekpneō*)
God speaks at Jesus' baptism: "You are my beloved Son"	Centurion at the cross: "Truly this man was the Son of God"

What these elements illustrate is that Jesus' baptism in Mark 1 is the commencement of His ministry and mission. The prophecy of Daniel 9:24–27 reaches a crucial point with the completion of the sixty-ninth prophetic week at Jesus' baptism in AD 27. His ministry culminates at the cross three and a half years later, bringing in "everlasting righteousness" (verse 24). Mark highlights this culmination with the parallelism of five characteristics. John the Baptist baptizes Jesus, and Jesus points to the cross as His baptism (Mark 10:38). John the Baptist is an Elijah-like figure (cf. Mark 9:11–13), and the bystanders at the cross think that Jesus is calling Elijah. The heavens split for the descent of the Spirit at the baptism, and the veil is split at Jesus' death (the only two uses in Mark of the verb *schizō*, "to split"). The Spirit descends on Jesus at His baptism, and when He dies, the verb Mark uses to describe His death is *ekpneō*, "to expire," which contains the root for the word "Spirit," *Pneuma*, within it. And God speaks at Jesus' baptism, "You are my beloved Son" (Mark 1:11), while the centurion at the cross says, "Truly this man was the Son of God!" (Mark 15:39). All these details, put together, help us to see the centrality of the cross.

Laid to rest

The death of Jesus was the end of the disciples' faith and the disappointment of their high hopes in following Him. It is remarkable that an unexpected man appeared on the scene to oversee the burial of Jesus—Joseph of Arimathea. Mark tells us that he was a member of the council who condemned Jesus and that he was looking for the kingdom of God. Nowhere in the Gospels are we told whether Joseph was present at Jesus' trial.[11] The fact that he came forward to bury Jesus strongly suggests that he was not.

Joseph took upon himself the risk of association with a man executed for sedition against the Romans, thus the reference that he "took courage and went to Pilate and asked for the body of Jesus" (verse 43). Pilate was surprised that Jesus was already dead since it often took days for someone to die on a cross. He sent for the centurion, who certified that Jesus was dead. This is an important detail that counters those who argue that Jesus only fainted. Two women are noted in the scene—Mary Magdalene and Mary, the mother of Joses. These two women became witnesses to the empty tomb, so their presence at Jesus' burial adds to the historical character of the events.

---

1. See Mark L. Strauss, *Mark*, Zondervan Exegetical Commentary on the New Testament (Grand Rapids, MI: Zondervan, 2014), 673.

2. See Colin M. Wells, "Roman Empire," in *The Anchor Bible Dictionary*, ed. David Noel Freedman (New Haven, CT: Yale University Press, 1992), 5:805.

3. See Flavius Josephus, *Jewish War* 2.9.4; Flavius Josephus, *Antiquities of the Jews* 18.3.2. See also Craig A. Evans, *Mark 8:27–16:20*, Word Biblical Commentary 34B (Nashville, TN: Thomas Nelson, 2001), 476–478.

4. Strauss, *Mark*, 679, 680, note 32. See also Raymond E. Brown, *The Death of the Messiah*, Anchor Bible Reference Library (New York: Doubleday, 1994), 1:851–853.

5. See Brown, *Death of the Messiah*, 1:248, 701, 864, 865. Evans argues for a more variable two hundred to six hundred men. See Evans, *Mark 8:27–16:20*, 489, 490. Also see Strauss, *Mark*, 687.

6. Seneca, *Ad Lucilium* 101.14. See Strauss, *Mark*, 691.

7. See Raymond E. Brown, *The Death of the Messiah*, Anchor Bible Reference Library (New York: Doubleday, 1994), 2:952, 953.

8. William D. Edwards, Wesley J. Gabel, and Floyd E. Hosmer, "On the Physical Death of Jesus Christ," *Journal of the American Medical Association* 255, no. 11 (March 21, 1986): 1455–1463. See also Brown, *Death of the Messiah*, 2:1088–1092.

9. See Strauss, *Mark*, 691.

10. Ellen G. White, *The Desire of Ages* (Mountain View, CA: Pacific Press®, 1940), 753.

11. Ellen White indicates that he and Nicodemus were not present. *The Desire of Ages*, 699.

13

The Risen Lord

Open a modern version of the Bible to Mark 16, and you will find twenty verses, as in most earlier versions. But there will be a note, either in the text or in a footnote, indicating that some of the earliest manuscripts do not include verses 9–20. In fact, some manuscripts have a short addition to verse 8, called the "Shorter Ending"; others include verses 9–20, called the "Longer Ending." Which ending is the correct one?

The earliest manuscript of Mark comes from the third century AD—a papyrus known as Papyrus 45 ($\mathfrak{P}^{45}$). Unfortunately, it does not extend past Mark 12:28. After that, the two oldest Greek manuscripts that contain the ending of Mark are Codex Sinaiticus and Codex Vaticanus, which are excellent manuscripts from the fourth century AD. Neither of these two manuscripts goes past Mark 16:8. But there are many other manuscripts that include verses 9–20; the oldest of these comes from the fifth century AD.

How do we decide which one of these endings is the correct one? The New Testament is far and away the best-attested document from the ancient world. We have what Daniel Wallace, a well-known textual scholar, calls "an embarrassment of riches."[1] That is, there are so many manuscripts—more than three thousand—that it is challenging to determine which reading is best. Scholars have developed a set of logical rules that, carefully applied, bring us to greater certainty as to what the Bible writers actually wrote. Kurt Aland and Barbara Aland, two of the most respected New Testament textual scholars of the twentieth century, put it this way:

> The transmission of the New Testament textual tradition is characterized by an extremely impressive degree of *tenacity*. Once a reading occurs it will persist with obstinacy. It is precisely the overwhelming mass of the New Testament textual tradition, . . . which provides an assurance of certainty in establishing the original text. . . . We can be certain that among these [all the manuscripts] there is still a group of witnesses which preserves the original form of the text, despite the pervasive authority of ecclesiastical tradition and the prestige of the later text.[2]

This is an amazing statement. It illustrates that we can be certain about the text of the New Testament.

So, returning to the ending of Mark, what do the rules of textual criticism point to as the ending of the Gospel? Here is the data. The two earliest Greek manuscripts with Mark 16 end the book at verse 8. We have a few versions from the fourth through the seventh centuries that add the Shorter Ending to Mark 16:8. Then there is a larger group of witnesses from the third through thirteenth centuries that add both the Shorter Ending and the Longer Ending to Mark 16:8. Finally, most witnesses have Mark 16:8 and the Longer Ending—verses 9–20. The Greek manuscripts of this group range from the fifth through the fourteenth centuries, and the versions range from the third to the fourth centuries, with many Greek church fathers and a few Latin church fathers affirming it.

What are we to make of this data? Certainly, the manuscripts with verses 1–20 are the most numerous. But it is interesting that we have two different types of versions of the text that go beyond verse 8 (Shorter Ending and Longer Ending), and we have some manuscripts that include both! That means the scribes who were copying the text had in front of them manuscripts that had the Shorter Ending or the Longer Ending, and the scribe included both. This is a prime example of that idea of tenacity.

It is challenging to argue that a Christian scribe would cut away verses 9–20 or even the Shorter Ending from the text, especially with the way verse 8 ends with the women going away and telling no one. So we are left with the fairly clear alternative that the Gospel of Mark originally ended at Mark 16:8. But why would the Evangelist end his Gospel in this way?

A surprise ending

Ever since the beginning of the Gospel of Mark, the reader has known that Jesus is the Messiah: "The beginning of the gospel of Jesus Christ, the Son of God" (Mark 1:1). In comparison, throughout most of the book, the disciples seem rather dense and slow to learn who Jesus is and where He is headed. They do not like His predictions about the cross and are loath to ask Him about them. During His Passion, they fail miserably and run away from Him, and Peter denies Him three times. Compared to us, they seem somewhat inadequate in their knowledge, and quite a few people might see them as insufficient emissaries of the gospel message.

This sense of inadequacy continues after the Crucifixion. The disciples are not there to bury Jesus; a rich man does it instead, with a few women watching. These women catch our attention as they purchase spices after the close of the Sabbath with the intention of going to the tomb on Sunday morning to anoint Jesus' body (verse 1).

But even these women may come across as unprepared for what they intend to do, since they question each other as to who will remove the stone from Jesus' tomb (verse 3). But to their surprise, the stone is already rolled away (verse 4). Entering the tomb, they encounter a "young man" in a white robe who knows what their errand is, what has happened, and what they are supposed to do (verses 5–7). He tells them that Jesus has risen, that He is going before them to Galilee, where they will see Him, and that they are supposed to go and tell the disciples and Peter about this. What do they do? They run away in silence and tell no one because they are afraid!

This seems like an odd way to end the Gospel story. What is going on? First, we must explain the characteristics of the scene. This scene, like a number of scenes in Scripture, is called a *theophany*, or an epiphany, which means the appearance of God or a heavenly being to human beings. Such an epiphany has five characteristics:

1. The heavenly being appears with glory.
2. The people are afraid.
3. The heavenly visitor says, "Do not fear."
4. There is a revelation from the heavenly visitor.
5. The humans respond to the revelation.

A typical example of this is the birth of Jesus in Luke 2. The shepherds are watching over their sheep at night.

- Point 1: The angel of the Lord appears with glory.
- Point 2: The shepherds are afraid.
- Point 3: The angel says, "Do not be afraid."

- Point 4: Then the angel shares the message of the birth of Jesus.
- Point 5: Then the shepherds respond by going to see the Baby Jesus.

These same five characteristics appear in Mark's story of the Resurrection.

- Point 1: The heavy stone has been rolled away, and there is a young man in the tomb who knows all that has happened.
- Point 2: The women are afraid.
- Point 3: The "young man," quite clearly an angel, says, "Do not be alarmed."
- Point 4: The young man tells them why they have come, what has happened, and what they are to do.
- Point 5: The women run away in fear and tell no one.

It all fits perfectly, except for that last point. Why would they tell no one? It is part of the revelation-secrecy motif that runs throughout the Gospel of Mark, where Jesus typically tells people not to say anything about a miracle or about who He is. For example, the healed leper (Mark 1:44), Jairus and his wife (Mark 5:43), the people who see Jesus heal a deaf and mute man (Mark 7:36), and His own disciples (Mark 8:30) are all instructed not to tell who He is.

At the same time, Jesus' power is often revealed. He casts out a demon in Capernaum's synagogue (Mark 1:21–28), He heals a man's withered hand in the synagogue (Mark 3:1–6), He heals a demon-possessed man who goes about proclaiming what Jesus did for Him (Mark 5:19, 20), and He heals the woman with the hemorrhage, placing the whole truth on display before everyone (verse 33).

We have seen before that when Jesus tells people not to

tell something, they usually go and tell anyway. Now here in Mark 16, the women are told to go and tell, and they run away in fear and tell no one. The consistent feature in these encounters is that people do not do what they are told! What are we to make of this detail, particularly in Mark 16, where it is a reversal from "do not tell" to "go and tell"?

An analogy can help at this point. Parents and grand-parents like to read bedtime stories to their children and grandchildren. It is a wonderful bedtime routine that builds relationships and allows the older generation to share character values. It is common for a parent to say to the child, "You choose the book you want me to read to you." Lo and behold, the child chooses the *same book* he or she has chosen every night for a long time. If the parent says, "Wouldn't you like to read a different book?" The answer is typically, "No, I like this one."

Sometimes that gets to the parent, and the parent does something to change things up—perhaps skipping a page or changing the ending. I have had the personal experience of skipping a page by error, whereupon the child turns the page back to hear the entire story. If I change the ending, the child will say, "Daddy, that is not how the story ends. Tell it the right way." We can learn important lessons from children.

Here is what is happening at the end of the Gospel of Mark. Running away in fear and telling no one is "not how the story ends." The women did not tell. Someone has to go and tell. And who will that be? You, the reader.

All through Mark, the reader has been "above" the characters in the story in terms of knowledge about Jesus and where the story is headed. This can create a sense of superiority. But here, at the end of the book, the Evangelist changes the situation with an open ending to the story, thus making an appeal to the reader. Obviously, someone did tell, but Mark leaves that open and unexplained, challenging the reader to be the one who goes and shares the good news about Jesus' death and resurrection.

The ending of Mark and the end of the story

We can see how this information concerning the open ending of Mark 16 fits with the revelation-secrecy motif that runs throughout the entire book. If the book ends at Mark 16:8, the secrecy aspect of the motif comes to a climax, with a covert appeal to the reader to go and tell the good news. This conclusion then agrees with the textual decision we saw that scholars have come to regarding the different endings of Mark—Mark 16:8 is the most likely ending of the book. If the literary data agrees with the textual data, we have a stronger case for where the book most likely ends, as written by the Evangelist.

But this may trouble some who have read Mark 16:9–20 for a long time and believe it to be the actual ending of the book. For such people, there is solace in the way that the Longer Ending was written. The Longer Ending has parallels throughout the New Testament as follows:

1. Mark 16:9–11: Jesus appeared first to Mary Magdalene; Luke 24:9–11; John 20:1–18
2. Mark 16:12, 13: Jesus appeared to two in the country; Luke 24:13–35
3. Mark 16:14: Jesus appeared to the Eleven; Luke 24:36–43; John 20:19, 24–29
4. Mark 16:15: Jesus commissions the disciples to preach; Matthew 28:19, 20
5. Mark 16:16: The believer saved, and the unbeliever condemned; John 3:18; Acts 2:38; 1 Peter 3:21
6. Mark 16:17: Signs of believers are casting out demons and speaking new tongues; Acts 2:1–13; 16:16–18; Hebrews 2:4

7. Mark 16:18: Believers can pick up snakes and heal the sick; Acts 28:1–10
8. Mark 16:19: Jesus ascends to the right hand of God; Acts 1:9–11; 2:32, 33; Ephesians 1:20, 21
9. Mark 16:20: The apostles preach, and signs follow; Acts 1:8; Colossians 1:23; Hebrews 2:3, 4

We can think of the Longer Ending like this: Mark the Evangelist did such a good job in writing an open ending to his Gospel that someone in the second century said, "That is not how the story ends! That is no way to end a Gospel!" And that person put together an ending in keeping with the other writings of the nascent New Testament circulating among Christians and appended that to Mark 16:8.

An open ending?

One more point should be made. Some modern readers may find that Mark 16:8 is too sophisticated of an open ending for an ancient document. Would the Evangelist really have the literary skill to tell the story in this way, impelling the reader to "go and tell"? The information above suggests that the answer is yes. But we also have corroboration from other open-ended stories in the Bible itself. The parable of the prodigal son is open-ended. Did the older brother go inside the house? The book of Jonah is open-ended. How did Jonah respond to God's question? Did Jonah repent? The book of Acts is open-ended. What happened to Paul?

Each of these examples of open endings has a purpose. The parable of the prodigal son is an appeal to the Pharisees. Will they welcome sinners home? The book of Jonah is an appeal to Israel to look beyond its borders to bless the surrounding nations. The ending of the book of Acts implies that the mission is not ended—it is still going forward.

And so, the Gospel of Mark ends with an appeal to the

reader to go and tell the good news: Jesus is risen from the dead! Tell it to all the nations.

1. Daniel B. Wallace, "An Interview With Daniel B. Wallace on the New Testament Manuscripts," interview by Justin Taylor, *Gospel Coalition* (blog), March 22, 2012, https://www.thegospelcoalition.org/blogs/justin-taylor/an-interview-with-daniel-b-wallace-on-the-new-testament-manuscripts/.

2. Kurt Aland and Barbara Aland, *The Text of the New Testament*, trans. Erroll F. Rhodes (Grand Rapids, MI: Eerdmans, 1987), 286, 287; emphasis in the original.